GOD
THE
FATHER

OVERTURES TO BIBLICAL THEOLOGY

A series of studies in biblical theology designed to explore fresh dimensions of research and to suggest ways in which the biblical heritage may address contemporary culture

Editors

WALTER BRUEGGEMANN, Dean of Academic Affairs and Professor of Old Testament at Eden Theological Seminary

JOHN R. DONAHUE, S.J., Associate Professor of New Testament at Vanderbilt Divinity School

*Theology
and
Patriarchy
in the
Teaching of Jesus*

GOD
THE
FATHER

ROBERT HAMERTON-KELLY

FORTRESS PRESS   Philadelphia

COPYRIGHT © 1979 BY FORTRESS PRESS

Library of Congress Cataloging in Publication Data

Hamerton-Kelly, Robert.
God the Father.

(Overtures to Biblical theology)
Includes index.
1. God—Biblical teaching. 2. Bible. N.T.—
Theology. 3. Jesus Christ—Teachings. I. Title.
II. Series.
BS544.H35   231   78-54551
ISBN 0-8006-1528-X

7128F78   Printed in the United States of America   1-1528

for
CHRISTOPHER NGUYEN
my adopted son

Contents

Series Foreword

Biblical theology has been a significant part of modern study of the Jewish and Christian Scriptures. Prior to the ascendancy of historical criticism of the Bible in the nineteenth century, biblical theology was subordinated to the dogmatic concerns of the churches, and the Bible too often provided a storehouse of rigid proof texts. When biblical theology was cut loose from its moorings to dogmatic theology to become an enterprise seeking its own methods and categories, attention was directed to what the Bible itself had to say. A dogmatic concern was replaced by an historical one so that biblical theology was understood as an investigation of what was believed by different communities in different situations. By the end of the nineteenth century biblical theology was virtually equated with the history of the religion of the authors who produced biblical documents or of the communities which used them.

While these earlier perspectives have become more refined and sophisticated, they still describe the parameters of what is done in the name of biblical theology—moving somewhere between the normative statements of dogmatic theology and the descriptive concerns of the history of religions. Th. Vriezen, in his *An Outline of Old Testament Theology* (Dutch, 1949; ET, 1958), sought to combine these concerns by devoting the first half of his book to historical considerations and the second half to theological themes. But even that effort did not break out of the stalemate of categories. In more recent times Old Testament theology has been dominated by two paradigmatic works. In his *Theology of the Old Testament* (German, 1933–39; ET, 1967) W. Eichrodt has provided a comprehensive statement around fixed categories which reflect classical dogmatic interests, although the centrality of covenant in his work reflects the Bible's own categories. By contrast, G. von Rad in his *Old Testament Theology* (German, 1960; ET, 1965) has presented a study of theological traditions with a primary concern for the historical dynamism of the traditions. In the case of New Testament theology, historical and theological concerns are rather roughly juxtaposed in the work of A. Richardson, *An Introduction to the Theology of the New Testament.* As in the case of the Old Testament there are two major options or presentations which dominate in New Testament studies. The history-of-religion school has left its mark on the magisterial work of R. Bultmann, who proceeds from an explanation of the expressions of faith of the earliest communities and their theologians to a statement of how their understanding of existence under faith speaks to us today. The works of O. Cullmann and W. G. Kümmel are clear New Testament statements of *Heilsgeschichte* under the aegis of the tension between promise and fulfillment—categories reminiscent of von Rad.

As recently as 1962 K. Stendahl again underscored the tension between historical description and normative meaning by assigning to the biblical theologian the task of describing what the Bible *meant,* not what it *means* or *how* it can have meaning. However, this objectivity of historical description is too often found to be a mirror of the observer's hidden preunderstanding, and the adequacy of historical description is contingent on one generation's discoveries and postulates. Also, the yearning and expectation of believers and would-be believers will not let biblical theology rest with the descriptive task alone. The growing strength of Evangelical Protestantism and the expanding phenomenon of charismatic Catholicism are but vocal reminders that people seek in the Bible a source of alternative value systems. By its own character and by the place it occupies in our culture the Bible will not rest easy as merely an historical artifact.

Thus it seems a fitting time to make "overtures" concerning biblical theology. It is not a time for massive tomes which claim too much. It appears not even to be a time for firm conclusions which are too comprehensive. It is a time for pursuit of fresh hints, for exploration of new intuitions which may reach beyond old conclusions, set categories, and conventional methods. The books in this series are concerned not only with what is seen and heard, with what the Bible said, but also with what the Bible says and the ways in which seeing and hearing are done.

In putting forth these *Overtures* much remains unsettled. The certainties of the older biblical theology *in service* of dogmatics, as well as of the more recent biblical theology movement *in lieu* of dogmatics, are no longer present. Nor is there on the scene anyone of the stature of a von Rad or a Bultmann to offer a synthesis which commands the theological engagement of a generation and summons the church to a new restatement of the biblical message. In a period characterized by an information explosion the relation of analytic study to attempts at synthesis is unsettled. Also unsettled is the question whether the scholarly canon of the university or the passion of the confessing community provides a language and idiom of discourse, and equally unsettled—and unsettling—is the question whether biblical theology is simply one more specialization in an already fragmented study of scripture or whether it is finally the point of it all.

But much remains clear. Not simply must the community of biblical scholars address fresh issues and articulate new categories for the well-being of our common professional task; equally urgent is the fact that the dominant intellectual tradition of the West seems now to carry less conviction and to satisfy only weakly the new measures of knowing which are among us. We do not know exactly what role the Bible will play in new theological statements or religious postures, nor what questions the Bible can and will address, but *Overtures* will provide a locus where soundings may be taken.

We not only intend that *Overtures* should make contact with people professionally involved in biblical studies, but hope that the series will speak to all who care about the heritage of the biblical tradition. We hope that the volumes will represent the best in a literary and historical study of biblical traditions without canonizing historical archaism. We hope also that the studies will be relevant without losing the mystery of biblical religion's historical distance, and that the studies touch on significant themes, motifs, and symbols of the Bible without losing the rich diversity of the biblical tradition. It is a time for normative literature which is not heavy-handed, but which seriously challenges not only our conclusions but also the shape of our questions.

Hamerton-Kelly's study of *God the Father* represents an important overture to contemporary culture and theology. A near century of psychoanalytic research and reflection on the cultural importance of traditional symbols has shown us that the term "father" is both more significant and often more problematic than prior generations explicitly realized. The use of "god language" is a problem which continues to surface in different forms and with varying degrees of intensity. In our generation the description of God as Father and the possibilities which this symbol may offer for a vibrant religious life are, for many people, painful and urgent manifestations of the problem of speaking and thinking about God.

The present volume offers a multidimensional approach to this dominant biblical symbol. On the historical and descriptive level the work offers a picture of the origin and use of the image of God as Father in Israel's faith, in the experience and teaching of Jesus, and the early traditions about him. In offering an interpretation of these texts, Hamerton-Kelly adopts the evocative insights which Paul Ricoeur offers to biblical critics and shows that the symbol, father, has, at times, surprising dimensions of meaning which contravene both our initial preconceptions and surface reading of the biblical texts.

The author brings a very special set of competencies to his enterprise. He is a recognized authority on New Testament Christology and has been a professor at a major theological seminary. At present he is Dean of the Chapel at Stanford University. Here, he is engaged in mediating the biblical texts and symbols through the preached word and in listening to how these symbols touch the lives of people of our day. The present work invites the reader to become part of a similar experience of objective scholarly reflection on biblical texts and of a living and serious engagement with their meaning.

WALTER BRUEGGEMANN
JOHN R. DONAHUE, S.J.

Abbreviations

IDB	*Interpreter's Dictionary of the Bible*
JAAR	*Journal of the American Academy of Religion*
JBL	*Journal of Biblical Literature*
1 QH	The Scroll of the Thanksgiving Hymns from Qumran
Str-B	H. L. Strack and P. Billerbeck, *Kommentar zum neuen Testament aus Talmud und Midrasch*
TDNT	*Theological Dictionary of the New Testament*
Tg. Yer.	Targum Jerusalem I (an Aramaic translation of the Pentateuch made in the four centuries prior to the birth of Christ, also known as Targum Jonathan or Pseudo-Jonathan)

Preface

The first draft of this work was written during a six-month sojourn in Munich from April to September 1977. During that time my family and I experienced great kindness and warm hospitality from many people. Professor Wolfhart Pannenberg and his wife gave generously of their time, and cared for us with genuine solicitude. Their home was often open to us, and their friendship sustained us in many ways. The good people of the Church of the Ascension, led by Father Hank Wilson and his wife, Flo, were essential to our well-being, as a community of worship and friendship. Bob and Kristi Nowak were also important, and Kristi Nowak, Ph.D. read part of the draft for intelligibility. My colleagues at Stanford, the Rev. Wendy Smith, Ph.D., and the Rev. Ernlé Young, Ph.D. made my leave possible by caring for our church in my absence, and they, along with countless Stanford students, contributed insights and helped to clarify parts of the argument. An earlier draft of the work was delivered as the Lois Lewis Memorial lectures at St. Mark's Episcopal Church in Palo Alto; I thank Fr. Underwood and the parish for the invitation and the hospitality. The Alexander von Humboldt Stiftung provided part of the financial support for our stay in Munich, and Stanford University provided the rest. I thank the Stiftung and Richard Lyman, president of Stanford, for this. My wife helped in many ways, not least of which were the many discussions which helped me clarify murky concepts. John Donahue, S.J., was a careful and perceptive editor, whose work and knowledge have improved the volume greatly. To all of the above I owe grateful thanks, and especially to Wolfhart Pannenberg, who has been a help in this specific work, and, in general, an inspiration, an example and a friend.

ROBERT HAMERTON-KELLY

The Feast of the Ascension 1978

CHAPTER 1

The Father Figure

THE PROBLEM

In this study we understand the word "theology" in its narrow sense, as the intellectual concern for the idea of God, and it is surely not news that the biblical idea of God is suffering a widespread loss of credibility. Indeed, ever since the Enlightenment it has been on the retreat from regions of public discourse, and today, according to much Protestant thought, inhabits the subjectivity of the believer as some impregnable fortress. The retreat into subjectivism has been abetted, in this century, by the rise of various existentialist philosophies which, despairing of finding significance in the objective, public world, urge us to seek meaning in ourselves. The relationships between existentialist and Christian thought have ranged from an explicit alliance, as in the case of Rudolf Bultmann's exposition of Christianity in the terms of Martin Heidegger's early philosophy,[1] to a general participation by theologians in the spirit of the times.

The spirit of the times may be variously described, but, whatever adjectives one chooses, they all converge in expressing our need to assert our human individuality, our subjective selves, in the midst of a society rationally organized for efficient production. We are required in such a society to subordinate our personal needs to the demands of the organization, and although a certain self-denial for the sake of cooperation is reasonable, many think it has gone so far as to rob people of their private selves. Our lives are organized by the demands of the machines we tend or the corporations we serve,

1. Still the best account in English is John Macquarrie, *An Existentialist Theology, A Comparison of Heidegger and Bultmann* (New York: Harper and Row, 1965).

1

rather than by the energy of personal purpose; our thoughts are created and controlled by the needs of the economy we obey—modern advcrtising is surely the greatest and most effective effort at thought control in the history of the species—rather than by our native curiosity and desire for wisdom. The thought of our times is the philosophy of the feeding trough. Therefore it is easy to understand why existentialist philosophers and theologians have withdrawn from the jostling and snuffling of the public forum, have stepped aside from the Gadarene rush, and sought truth in the inward parts. By refusing to explain their views in terms demanded by the forum, and insisting rather on subjective decision as a prerequisite for understanding them, these philosophers and theologians express what they believe is a justified scepticism about the ability of public reason to understand anything profound.

The theologians have good precedent for such an attitude in the traditional Protestant suspicion of reason, which goes back all the way to Martin Luther.[2] They also have ample justification in the triviality and sentimentality of so much culture-bound Christianity, in which people participate without conviction. The demand for decision engages the will at a deep level, and faith can begin to make a difference to the way a committed Christian lives and thinks. There is good reason, therefore, for the existentialist attitude.

However, despite precedent and practical justification, such a demand for decision, made without positive reference to the warrants and strictures of public reason, can be dangerous. The most vivid recent example of this danger is the German National Socialist movement. Joachim Fest suggests that the traditional orientation of a German's existence towards private things—"family happiness, the emotions aroused by nature, the quiet passions of the study"—made for a tenuous appreciation of the reality of the political world.[3] Unwillingness to enter the din of the forum left public power for those brash enough to pick it up. It also made Germans susceptible

2. "But in spiritual matters, human reasoning certainly is not in order; other intelligence, other skill and power, are requisite here—something to be granted by God himself and revealed through his Word." Epistle Sermon, Twelfth Sunday After Trinity; quoted by Hugh T. Kerr, *A Compend of Luther's Theology* (Philadelphia: Westminster, 1966) 3.

3. Joachim C. Fest, *Hitler,* trans. Richard and Clara Winston (Harmondsworth: Penguin, 1977; German edition, 1973) 563.

to the manipulations of the powerful, especially to the beguilements of "aesthetic politics" as practised by Hitler.[4] Hitler, his followers, and the whole nation fell victims to "the lack of grip upon reality characteristic of socially alienated intellectuals."[5] No more dire example of this loss of a grip on reality through an over-estimation of the competence of private thought can be found than the following quotation from Martin Heidegger. In November of 1933, Heidegger, in his capacity as rector of the University of Freiburg, proclaimed to the students: "Not doctrines and 'ideas' be the rules of your being. The Führer himself and alone is the present and future German reality and its law. Learn ever deeper to know: that from now on each and every thing demands decision, and every action responsibility. Heil Hitler!"[6] There is something seriously wrong with his premises when a man as intelligent as Heidegger comes to such catastrophic conclusions. "Decisionism," therefore, is no alternative to vulgar technological reason; it has its own "dark satanic mills."

We must attempt to think our way to an idea of God which gives each of these two alternatives its due, while not succumbing to their temptations. We must think with modest submission to the canons of common reason, and with a candid recognition of the demands for depth and resonance which our human nature makes upon the God idea. This is a task for theologians of all specializations, to which biblical theology must also make its contribution. Since the Bible speaks of God in symbols, part of biblical theology's contribution might be to elucidate the meaning of these symbols in our current cultural context. This is the hermeneutical task; to show what the Bible now means by what once it meant. We wish to share in the task of thinking towards an adequate idea of God by undertaking an examination of the symbol "Father" as applied to God in the teaching of Jesus. In so doing we do not intend to usurp the role of the systematician, but rather to make the raw materials of the bibli-

---

4. *Ibid.*, 566.

5. *Ibid.*, 568.

6. Quoted by Hans Jonas, "Heidegger and Theology," in *The Phenomenon of Life* (New York: Harper and Row, 1966) 247, n. 11. Jonas continues, ". . . neither then nor now did Heidegger's thought provide a norm by which to decide how to answer such calls . . . no norm except depth, resolution, and the sheer force of being that issues the call . . . As if the devil were not part of the voice of being!" (*ibid.*)

cal tradition available to him in a form slightly less raw than their primitive state.

The cultural context of the father figure is lively and confused. Behind all modern reflection on the subject stands the magisterial figure of Sigmund Freud. For him the father is the source of all morals and religion; every human being must work through his or her relationship to the father on the way to maturity. In *Moses and Monotheism*,[7] to which we shall return, Freud set forth for the last time his controversial thesis that behind religion and morals lies the memory of the murder of the father at the dawn of human history. Religion and morals are, in fact, merely ways in which the repressed memory of this deed finds expression. Thus the dead and repressed father, whose figure each one of us internalizes and thereby makes into a source of authority, is more powerful than the living one. Even though psychotherapy has moved beyond Freud's narrower theories in its practical work, his basic discoveries—of the subconscious and its strategies, and the self's capacity for self-deception—still command wide support. Indeed, Freud has experienced a revival in some French intellectual circles, and Paul Ricoeur has attempted recently to make Freud's thought bear fruit for the hermeneutical endeavor.[8] This suggests that we might profit from a Freudian look at the biblical texts.

However, the father may not be as central to our psychic life as Freud assumed. In an introduction to some papers from a three-year seminar on the father at the University of Heidelberg, in the early seventies, Hubertus Tellenbach, a well-known psychiatrist, writes that the father figure has all but vanished from the western psyche.[9] For the young schizophrenics whom he has seen in the course of a long practice, Tellenbach found that the father is a nonentity, and that the developmental phase of rebellion against the father is missing in most cases. He regards the vanishing of the father as the outcome of a long process, which can be traced in art and literature.

7. *The Standard Edition of the Complete Psychological Works of Sigmund Freud*, ed. James Strachey et al., vol. 23 (London: Hogarth, 1964).

8. Paul Ricoeur, *Freud and Philosophy, An Essay on Interpretation*, trans. Denis Savage (New Haven and London: Yale University, 1970).

9. Hubertus Tellenbach, herausg., *Das Vaterbild in Mythos und Geschichte* (Stuttgart: Kohlhammer, 1976). Cf. Leighton McCutchen, "The Father Figure in Psychology and Religion," *JAAR* 40 (1972) 176–192, who argues that the father is indeed present, but in a diffuse form.

In the middle ages God the Father was portrayed as equally young and virile as the Son (e.g. Wolfram von der Steinen). Beginning in the thirteenth century, however, God the Father began to appear as an old man, and by the nineteenth had died of old age and ineptitude (e.g. Nietzsche). The human father's progress paralleled God's, and in the nineteenth century he finally turned into an ineffectual clown (e.g. Dostoevski's *The Brothers Karamazov*). Tellenbach regards this absence of the father as one important cause of the youthful rebellion of the late sixties and early seventies, and sets his seminar the task of discovering whether a spark of the erstwhile glory of the father figure can be discovered in our flaccid consciousness and fanned into a flame by reflection on the place of that figure in our cultural heritage. Therefore, Freud's insistence on the father's centrality in human consciousness is not without serious challenge.

The most serious challenge, however, comes from the women's movement, which in its moderate form is seeking a reform of the church's language about God in theology and liturgy, and equal opportunity for women in the ministry; and in its radical feminist manifestation seeks nothing less than a total revision of the idea of God. Mary Daly is a brilliant spokesperson for the radical feminist position, and her book *Beyond God the Father*[10] cannot be ignored by anyone concerned with the idea of God in our time.

There is an ironic convergence between Daly and Freud, whose theory she execrates as the "hideous blossom" of the religions of patriarchy.[11] Both see the notion of God as Father to be the Achilles' heel of the Judeo-Christian religions. Freud picked this image as the loose thread which when tugged would unravel the neurotic cover that religion provides for atavistic sexual fears and guilts. The fatherhood of God was the badge of religion as a communal neurosis. Daly sees the father image as the cornerstone of a self-alienating mode of existence which produces rape, genocide and war. When the father-god and all his works are renounced, a new heaven and earth of mutual respect, truth and vitality will come about. She argues for a symbolization which is not anthropomorphic; ". . . neither the Father, nor the Son, nor the mother *is* God . . . [God is]

10. Mary Daly, *Beyond God the Father, Toward a Philosophy of Women's Liberation* (Boston: Beacon, 1973).
11. *Ibid.,* 149.

the Verb who transcends anthropomorphic symbolization . . ."[12] She argues that a revisioning of God must focus on the experience of becoming rather than the sense of structure and permanence, and in this emphasis acknowledges a certain affinity with theologians in the Whiteheadian tradition. However, she is careful to note that since her project is to be carried out by women and for women it is bound to be unprecedented, since women have not been allowed to establish any precedents in patriarchy.

One can only hope that Daly is right, and that the human race has finally found the cure for rape, genocide and war; that the second coming is at hand.[13] However, one may be excused a certain scepticism, because of the sweeping nature of her claims. It is not clear that everything wrong[14] with the human race can be attributed to the way in which society is organized, nor that women are the bearers of such goodness as Daly believes. To make "patriarchy" the root of all evil is comparable to the way the Marxists use "capital" in their analysis of the world's ills, and is a form of demonology. All ills simply cannot be attributed to one cause; patriarchy as the devil is not very helpful in analyzing the human dilemma. That it has contributed its share to the common malaise has been ably demonstrated by Daly, but there are many other factors to be included in the analysis. Perhaps the most puzzling such factor is the individual's perversity, the love of death and destruction that thwarts all attempts to organize human beings for goodness. Any analysis of the roots of our disease must balance the societal and the individual contributions.

We may question her larger claim, that the women's movement is the bearer of the world's salvation, but we cannot ignore Daly's challenge and promise: the challenge that the patriarchal shape of Judaism and Christianity has contributed mightily to the ills which these religions are committed to relieve; that the religions are, in short, self-contradictory; and that this is caused by their devotion to the symbol of "father" for God; the promise that when we move beyond the father symbol we shall enter new realms of energy and possibility for human happiness.

12. *Ibid.,* 97.
13. *Ibid.,* 95–6, 132 ff.
14. I take her "unholy trinity" of rape, genocide and war as representative of "everything wrong."

THE TASK

It seems timely, therefore, to look once again at the biblical use of the father symbol in the light of our current cultural situation. The Bible continues to exercise an enormous influence in our culture, especially in favor of the status quo. It is not without moment, therefore, when such scholars as Phyllis Trible,[15] John Otwell[16] and Paul Jewett[17] show that the Bible does not represent so harsh a patriarchy as the radical feminists believe. It seems worthwhile to pursue Krister Stendahl's question, "Does the New Testament contain elements, glimpses which point beyond and even 'against' the prevailing view and practice of the New Testament church?"[18] Before we venture "beyond God the Father" we should reflect again on the role of the father image in the Bible's theology, in the new light which comes from our changed culture.

PRESUPPOSITIONS OF THE METHOD

Since that culture is characterized not only by the radical feminist initiative, but also by a revival of Freudian theory and the vanishing of patriarchal power, we have chosen to approach the biblical material with the help of a working hypothesis based as broadly as possible in that culture. We take as our hypothesis Ricoeur's restatement of Freud's Oedipus theory, because it is still true that all discussion of the father in our time begins with Freud. Obviously this starting point will not satisfy the feminists, and will seem anachronistic to someone like Tellenbach who believes that our problem is the absence rather than the hidden presence of the father. Their strictures and warnings will make us sensitive to possible exaggerations in the application of the Oedipus theory. The chief effect of their criticism, however, is to make Oedipus merely a working hypothesis, while Freud regarded him to be a psychological truth. Before we give Ricoeur's restatement of the theory, we might refresh

15. "Depatriarchalizing in Biblical Interpretation," *JAAR* 41 (1973) 30–48; *God and the Rhetoric of Sexuality* (Philadelphia: Fortress, 1978) .

16. *And Sarah Laughed, The Status of Women in the Old Testament* (Philadelphia: Westminster, 1977) .

17. *Man as Male and Female, a Study in Sexual Relationships from a Theological Point of View* (Grand Rapids: Eerdmans, 1975) .

18. *The Bible and the Role of Women, a Case Study in Hermeneutics,* trans. Emilie T. Sander (Philadelphia: Fortress, 1966) 34.

our memory of Freud's own version, and his perception of its pertinence for Judaism and Christianity.

In *Moses and Monotheism,* Freud used his Oedipal thesis as a principle for interpreting the biblical accounts of the origin and nature of Judeo-Christian monotheism. His exposition is as follows: Moses was an aristocratic Egyptian who became an adherent of the solar monotheistic religion of Pharaoh Akhenaten (1375–1358 B.C.). When, after Akhenaten's death, the ancient polytheism reasserted itself and attempted to erase all signs of his heresy, Moses was governor of an eastern province (Goshen) in which certain Semitic tribes had settled. He persuaded these tribes to remain loyal to Akhenaten's monotheism and to follow him (Moses) out of Egypt in search of a land where they might practise their religion unmolested. In the course of the journey the people murdered Moses in an uprising against his authority (Sellin). They also linked up with other Semitic tribes and accepted the god of these tribes as identical with their own god. This new god was Yahweh, a volcano divinity associated with the Midianites and the oasis of Meribah Kadesh (Meyer). The arrangement between the Neo-Egyptians (as Freud calls these followers of Moses) and the Midianite Semites was a compromise; in return for identifying their god Aten with Yahweh, the Neo-Egyptians were allowed to make their founding leader Moses the great prophet of Yahweh, to introduce their sacred rite of circumcision, and to make the experience of the Exodus a part of the tradition. The one thing assiduously excluded from the religion was any reference to the murder of Moses.

Yahweh was a god of no great stature when the Neo-Egyptians embraced him at Kadesh. He differed little from a local godling or Baal. The Neo-Egyptians abandoned the monotheism and ethical austerity of Moses' god Aten, in favor of the magical immediacy of Yahweh's volcanic power. Nevertheless, in the course of time these abandoned traits of Moses' religion grew not weaker but stronger, and eventually triumphed in the hands of the great prophets, transforming Yahwism into an ethical monotheism. This remarkable persistence is to be explained by analogy with the individual's experience of a neurosis, which has the following stages: (i) the trauma, usually suffered in early childhood, is met by a defence which represses it; (ii) it leads a latent life until (iii) it breaks out in neurotic symptoms and the repressed material returns. In the group psychology of the people of Israel a similar process took place. They murdered Moses who was to them a father figure and then repressed the memory of the man and his god. The repressed material, however, returned in triumph later, and Moses' ethical monotheism defined the nature of Yahweh.

This process recapitulated an experience of the whole human race, according to Freud, an experience so fundamental and primitive that it gave rise not merely to the prophet but to the very god himself. Drawing on the theories of Darwin, Atkinson and Robertson Smith, Freud postulates that originally human beings lived in hordes ruled by a dominant male. This male possessed all the women, and kept his sons subjugated by murder, castration, or expulsion. In the course of time a group of expelled brothers united to overpower the father, whom they then devoured raw. They did this because, like modern neurotics, they both hated their father and admired him so much that they wanted to be identified with him; this they achieved by eating him. Then followed a period of dispute amongst the brothers since each wanted to occupy the father's position. When they realized the futility of such rivalry, they renounced "instinct," recognized mutual obligations, and set up sacred institutions. The chief renunciation each one made was of the right to possess his mother and sisters, the right to assume the father's role, and out of this renunciation arose the taboo on incest and the injunction to exogamy. Some of the power liberated by the removal of the father passed to the women and a period of matriarchy ensued which was, however, overtaken again by patriarchy in the course of time.

The brothers of this fraternal alliance set up the figure of a powerful animal in place of the murdered father. This animal was venerated most of the time as the tribe's ancestor and protector, but periodically it was slaughtered and eaten in a sacred "totem meal" (Robertson Smith), which celebrated the sons' victory over the father. Gradually, however, the animal which took the place of the father was humanized, the father returned. At first he reappeared uncertainly as the son alongside a great mother-goddess. The end of the process was the full return of the repressed primal father, to take up his absolute rule once again: and this return occurs as the establishment of monotheism.

Along with the primal father, however, comes the guilt at the memory of his murder. In order to deal with this the ringleader amongst the rebellious brothers, the first son, dies as their representative and thereby expiates the guilt of all. This son is the prototype of the hero, the one who rebels against his father and kills him. By a process which Freud does not explain but merely describes as characteristic of the "ambivalence that dominates the relation to the father,"[19] the sin-bearing son not only propitiates the father, but displaces him. "The old God the Father fell back behind Christ; Christ, the Son, took his place just as every son had hoped to do in primeval times."[20]

Monotheism made its impact on the Jews because their memory of the murder of their father figure Moses made them particularly susceptible to the return of the murdered and repressed primal father. The repetition of the primal crime awoke a forgotten memory-trace in the group-psychology of Israel, showing indeed that such traces of an archaic heritage do exist. The existence of these memory-traces is independently established by clinical evidence which shows that the individual shares in a common human heritage which stretches back to primal times. In religious doctrines, especially the monotheistic idea, two particular elements from this history are prominent:

> on the one hand fixations to the ancient history of the family and survivals of it, and on the other hand revivals of the past and returns after long intervals of what has been forgotten.[21]

The clinical evidence shows that "ontogeny (individual development) recapitulates phylogeny (the history of the species)"; and, Freud concludes, "After this discussion I have no hesitation in declaring that men have always known (in this special way) that they once possessed a primal father and killed him."[22] Monotheism and its concomitant moral power, apparently based on faith which "believes because it is absurd," is in fact based on the memory of the aggrieved primal father, whose will is to be obeyed all the more

19. *Moses and Monotheism,* 87.
20. *Ibid.,* 88.
21. *Ibid.,* 84.
22. *Ibid.,* 101. Cf. R. Paul, "Did the Primal Crime Take Place?" *Ethos* 4 (1976) 311–352.

assiduously because we have grieved him. The murdered father binds us to himself by our guilt.

We have summarized the argument of *Moses and Monotheism* because it is Freud's most mature statement of his views on the origin of religion and morals. It also sets out his presumption that there is an analogy between the psychic history of the individual on the one hand and of the group on the other. On the group level this history is expounded in the form of the legend of the primal crime; on the individual level it takes the form of the myth of Oedipus. This myth is a representative portrayal of the way the individual (ontogeny) repeats the historical experience of the race (phylogeny) by murdering (in fantasy) his own father and possessing his mother. We might refresh our memory of the myth in order to deepen our understanding of the working hypothesis we intend to use.

The Oedipus cycle in Greek mythology is an account of the war between parents and children, beginning with Tantalus who out of vanity serves his son Pelops as a meal to the gods in order to test their ability to know everything.[23] The gods pass the test and condemn Tantalus to his well-known fate: condemned in Hades to stand thirsty in a pool of water that receded when he tried to drink it, and hungry with a bunch of fruit hanging over him which receded when he tried to pick from it. The gods restore Pelops to life. Pelops, now wise about parental love, kills King Oenomaus in order to marry his daughter Hippodamia, of whom her father was too possessive. So we see the baleful effects of a parent's jealousy or possessiveness. Next we see sibling rivalry when Pelops' sons Atreus and Thyestes quarrel, and in order to avenge a wrong Atreus kills Thyestes' two sons and serves them to him as a meal. At this point Laius appears on the scene and Pelops gives him a home at his court. Laius, however, wrongs him by ravishing his illegitimate son Chrysippus. The oracle tells Laius that in punishment for this he will be killed by his own son. To forestall this he has his son Oedipus pierced through the ankles and his feet tied together; then he gives him to a shepherd to expose. Instead of doing that, the shepherd gives him to a friend who takes him to his king, at whose court he is raised. The oracle then tells the youthful Oedipus that

23. Bruno Bettelheim, *The Uses of Enchantment* (New York: Knopf, 1976) 196–198.

he will slay his father and marry his mother, to prevent which he leaves his home on the mistaken assumption that the folk who reared him are his parents. At a crossroads he slays his father Laius unawares, then wanders into Thebes where he solves the riddle of the Sphinx and so abates the plague. As a reward he marries Queen Jocasta his mother. When his incest is revealed he blinds himself and she commits suicide. The cycle goes on to tell of the mutual slaughter of his sons and the execution of Antigone his daughter, but enough has been said to show that the myth regards parental jealousy, parental possessiveness, sibling rivalry, and the correlates of these attitudes in the children as fatal. The parents are the devourers of their children and the children want either to replace or possess their parents sexually.

Freud claims that this myth sets out the relationships within the average family. To take the example of the male child: first he identifies with the father as the ideal of what he would like to be; then he realizes that most of all he would like to be his mother's lover, not merely identify with the father but replace him. At this point he comes up against culture's incest prohibition which derives from the 'primal crime' and coincides with a sense of guilt at desiring the death of the father; guilt which is triggered by fear of the father's revenge, the castration fear, but in fact arises from the primal crime. It is internalized, however, along with the father figure; he becomes the inner representative of the incest taboo, and thus the source of all moral authority and all guilt. The ultimate origin of the incest taboo itself, and thus of the superego which it forms when it causes the ego to internalize its prohibition in the shape of the father figure, remains the memory of the primal crime which we have already considered.

There is one feature of Freud's account of the impact of the father figure which does not fit this picture, namely the father as succorer, upon whom the child-adult depends with an infantile need for consolation; the "father complex" which is, for Freud, the essence of religion. This feature he explains by means of another line of deduction from the Oedipus fantasy, concerning the pleasure principle. The initial stage of this explanation is infant narcissism in which desire is omnipotent—the stage of "His Majesty the baby"; an early point in the progress away from infant narcissism occurs when the parents are perceived as sources for the fulfillment of desire; god is the great parent/provider. So religion is a step on the way from the pleasure principle to the reality principle; it abridges the omnipotence of desire, but mythologically. Ricoeur summarizes the "father complex" as follows:

> The father complex has indeed a double valency; on the one hand it forces one to abandon the position of infancy and thus it functions as law; but at the same time it holds any subsequent formation of ideals within the network of dependence, fear, prevention of punishment, desire for consolation. It is against the background of the archaism of a figure irremediably attached to our infancy that we must overcome, each in his own turn, the archaism of our desire.[24]

Freud's theory of the origin of monotheism poses an obvious problem for biblical faith in God the Father, namely, the problem of whether such a God is not, as Freud claims, merely the memory of an historical experience of the race, which is repeated by every individual in the family, and therefore, whether God the Father is only a human memory, rather than a divine being. Furthermore, one must ask whether such a memory is not harmful to human sanity, retarding psychological growth, and to morality, sapping our self-esteem and will to do right. Freud believed that rejection of the idea of a divine Father-God was essential for human maturity and sanity.

Paul Ricoeur, as we have already noted, has taken up Freud's challenge to biblical faith on two levels; the level of the process of interpreting the texts and the level of the substance of the texts themselves. He is concerned with the way symbols function in human experience, and his interest in Freud pertains to the idea that the unconscious dimension of thought has to be dealt with in any endeavor to ascertain the meaning of human communication.

Ricoeur's restatement of Freud occurs in an essay entitled "Fatherhood: From Phantasm to Symbol."[25] He argues that fatherhood is not a well-known, fixed concept, but rather an enigmatic and fluid one. It is "a process rather than a structure,"[26] "a designation that is susceptible to traversing a diversity of semantic levels, from the

---

24. *Freud and Philosophy*, 447.
25. *The Conflict of Interpretations, Essays in Hermeneutics* (Evanston: Northwestern University, 1974) 468–497.
26. *Ibid.*, 469.

phantasm of the father as castrater, who must be killed, to the symbol of the father who dies of compassion."[27] Initially, fatherhood resists becoming a symbol by virtue of being imbedded in the field of family relations (kinship), a field whose powerful rules bind the term to its absolutely literal significance of progenitor and ruler of the family. The distinction between phantasm and symbol shows that the figure is susceptible of extended meanings that are so different as to warrant different names: phantasm names the father figure as hostile and threatening, and the term implies that it is a pathological, untrue extension of meaning; symbol names the figure as producing a healthy response, and therefore as true. So the journey from phantasm to symbol is one from sickness to health, and from falsehood to truth.

The father figure is liberated from kinship bonds by the action upon it of other non-kinship figures which jog it loose. Thus the first step is a loss of identity, a renunciation of the initial image defined by kinship bonds by leaving the context of those bonds; and the last step is a return of the renounced kinship bonds at a higher level. Ricoeur tests this pattern of development by tracing the journey through three fields of awareness: psychoanalysis, the phenomenology of spirit, and the interpretation of the divine names—Freud, Hegel, and the Bible respectively. He believes that he can show that the vicissitudes of fatherhood are homologous on all three levels.

In field one, of the economy of desire, there are three stations on the way: the formation of the Oedipus complex, the destruction of the Oedipus complex, and the permanence of the Oedipus complex. For present purposes the Oedipus complex is summarized as the constitution of desire in its infantile omnipotence, meeting the father figure who opposes desire's megalomania and so has to be killed. The father threatens to castrate the child, and from this threat arises the child's desire to murder him. From this relationship proceed also the glorification of the killed father, the quest for reconciliation with his interiorized image, and the accumulation of guilt. Thus the Oedipus complex is formed—for everyone; it is our universal fate.

The complex is destroyed as a complex to the extent that it is

27. *Ibid.*, 468.

allowed to structure the psyche. This it does by its becoming the conscious recognition of the father as a distinct person, over against my psyche, rather than remaining an unconscious hatred of him. The "economy of all or nothing," of either/or, is destroyed, and the father is accepted as mortal, his immortality being seen as only "the fantastic projection of the omnipotence of desire."

However, at the third stage the Oedipus complex persists, albeit in a resolved form, insofar as it is one and the same desire that fuels our enthusiasm for the objects of culture ("those that the education of desire discloses to us"[28]) and our primitive megalomania. We take the same psychic energy which drives our hatred for and competitiveness with our father when we are in the throes of the unresolved Oedipus complex and use it to drive our devotion to the aesthetic and altruistic objects and ends of culture. The energy that sustains nobility is the energy of Oedipal malice transformed. Agape and Eros are the same love. Once the omnipotence of desire has been renounced by the acceptance of the father as a mortal person distinct from ourselves, the Oedipal energy is transformed, desire is set free for education. The education, however, still takes place within the sphere of the Oedipus complex, and so liberated desire which was freed by renunciation of omnipotence is in fact the return of the repressed father phantasm transformed into the mortal father symbol.

As the mortal father symbol rather than a phantasm produced by the unresolved Oedipal complex, the father figure, when used as a symbol for God, presents not an omnipotent and remote stranger but a figure to whom one relates as to an equal and a friend. We hope to show in what follows, that this third stage of "free" relationship to God is what the Bible means by the term "faith," and therefore, that the "father symbol" in the Bible has the force of "a mortal father symbol" rather than a phantasm produced by the craving for omnipotence.

That there is conscious recognition between father and son points to the next level on which the process of the father figure is to be recapitulated, that of the phenomenology of spirit. Here the stages are: the master/slave relationship, in which father and son are bound together as two self-consciousnesses; the realm of the "right"

28. *Ibid.*, 472.

(*Recht*) in which they are bound as two wills who compromise their desire for possession by means of the concepts of contract and property; and the family, founded in the spiritual substance of the ethical, beyond abstract right, the family which makes fatherhood possible. Ricoeur resorts to Hegel because he finds in him "concrete reflection," that is, a repetition of the acts by which the self-consciousness of humanity is expressed and constituted, with a view to possessing that self-consciousness again; a repetition which is "concrete" because it proceeds by interpreting the signs which self-consciousness has produced in the history of culture. Having traced the three stages of fatherhood in the history of individual desire, Ricoeur has now traced them in the history of communal desire, called the history of spirit or self-consciousness in general.

Finally, Ricoeur attempts to show that in the biblical traditions, which are exemplars of the religious stage of reflection, tracing the history of God-consciousness rather than self-consciousness, fatherhood repeats its three-stage pilgrimage. We meet the figure first as an absence rather than a presence: father has been overshadowed as a designation for God in the earliest narrative traditions by redeemer, lawgiver, the bearer of the name without a corresponding image, and the creator. Against the background of the ancient Near East, where the gods were assumed, as a matter of course, to be the fathers of their devotees, in the sense of progenitor, the austerity of the Bible's understanding is striking. God is related to his people as liberator and lawgiver, as the nameless one, mysteriously active in their experience, never as progenitor. The categories drawn from the world of the family are never used to describe God at the earliest levels of biblical tradition. Indeed, the term "creator" is an explicit rejection of all hints of a sexual element in God's relation to the world. If we understand the ancient Near Eastern idea of God as progenitor to correspond to the first Oedipal stage, of the formation of the complex, the universal fate of the race, then the Bible enters the process at the beginning of the second stage, the stage of its destruction, and goes on to the third stage, of its return at a new level. The Bible enters where the father (progenitor) is renounced, and the father figure is jogged loose from the world of kinship by means of other images like liberator and lawgiver. This early stage of renunciation is followed by the return of the father figure, a return which takes place in the prophetic traditions, in three literary forms, namely, designation, declaration, and invocation. We shall refer to these categories of Ricoeur from time to time in our exposition as a convenient way of classifying the various forms in which the return of the father figure occurs. However, they are not adequate to describe the full nature of the evidence; in fact, as we shall see, they are only marginally helpful.

For our purposes, the most helpful contribution Ricoeur makes in this article is the description of the Oedipus complex. It has three ingredients: formation, destruction, and persistence. We all form such a complex, and if we are to reach maturity, we must also destroy it and then accept the fact that it will return to persist on a new level. This "streamlined" version is the one we shall take for our working hypothesis.

Ricoeur applies the hypothesis to the biblical evidence as a whole, taking in the panorama of biblical literature at a glance and classifying the role of the father figure in the whole, by means of the Oedipus hypothesis. This procedure is vulnerable at one particular point, namely, in positing stage one on the basis of an argument from silence. The silence about God as Father in the early traditions may not be a pregnant silence; God as liberator and lawgiver may not have been alternatives to a renounced father image, but rather in and for themselves the primary categories by which Israel understood God. Ricoeur has brought the Oedipus hypothesis with him to the biblical evidence, and because he finds stages two and three present, he posits stage one, relying presumably upon an estimate of the hypothesis as high as Fr. Pohier's, which holds that there is no place for religion "outside the field structured by the Oedipus complex."[29] The striking disavowal of the paternity of God is a factor in favor of the presumption that there was something substantial to disavow; but that "something substantial" could have been the doctrines of divine paternity in rival ancient Near Eastern religions, and not a universal state of Oedipal involvement with the father. If the objection is sustained, then we have no grounds for speaking of the Oedipus theme in connection with the father image in the Bible, for we have only two elements: an inferred renunciation of divine paternity, and a use of the father figure to symbolize God. It would, however, be overly austere to forbid Ricoeur to presup-

29. As quoted by Ricoeur, *ibid.*, 473.

pose the formation of the Oedipus complex as a background to the renunciation we observe, and so we conclude that such an objection can be sustained only at the cost of imagination, and find Ricoeur vulnerable but not defeated in his grand scheme.

We, in any case, propose taking a more modest, closer look at the evidence, seeking not a grand overview but rather the understanding of the father symbol from passage to passage. If we discover all three stages of the Oedipus experience in several individual passages, Ricoeur's presupposition will receive further justification. If the thesis enables us to see the meaning of the texts more clearly, it will obviously be validated for those parts of the biblical tradition.

The questions we are seeking to answer are the ones asked by Freud, and, in a different context, by Mary Daly. Is the God of the Bible merely a phantasm produced by the memory of the murder of the father in primal time and reexperienced in every individual's struggle to break the umbilical cord and establish an independent identity from the parents? If the biblical God, especially when presented by the father symbol, can be shown to provoke the responses typical of the unresolved Oedipal complex—hatred masked as love, rebellion cloaked as submission—then Freud's hypothesis is strengthened if not vindicated, and Daly's criticism of the God of the patriarchy is justified to that extent. If, however, the Bible portrays a relationship of mature freedom, typical of the resolved Oedipus complex, then some other estimate of that God is called for. Freud's claim that the God-relationship as such is inimical to personal growth and maturity cannot be sustained, and Daly's thesis that the biblical God epitomizes an authoritarianism which leads to rape, genocide, and war needs to be modified or even abandoned.

Ricoeur describes the contrast between Freud's unresolved Oedipal father-god and the Bible's resolved Oedipal father-god as that between phantasm and symbol. We believe he is essentially right in this matter and offer this study as a demonstration of that correctness based on a more careful consideration of the evidence—especially the teaching of Jesus—than Ricoeur could present in one brief article.

SYMBOL AND HISTORY

Since "father" is a symbol for God in the traditions we shall be examining, a preliminary explanation of our understanding of symbol is in order here. It is perforce preliminary because a full discussion would delay the exposition too much, and so has been relegated to an excursus at the end.[30] Nevertheless, a summary is adequate to orient the reader for the subsequent chapters.

In our understanding of symbol, we take our cue from Ricoeur once again.[31] A symbol is a sense unit with a double meaning, one surface meaning and one deeper meaning. The deeper meaning can only be reached through the surface meaning, by "dwelling in it" in thought and allowing the surface meaning to point thought to the deeper level. It cannot be gotten around, as if the symbol were merely one optional means of access to a meaning that could be directly grasped by discursive reasoning. There are certain dimensions of experience that are only accessible through symbols.

The biblical traditions we shall be examining are historical and not psychological, and therefore the deep meaning of our biblical symbol will be primarily historical rather than psychological. We do not expect it to disclose timeless truths about the human psyche directly, but rather hidden dimensions of human experience in history, which subsequently might be recognized as true presentations of the structure of the psyche. However, since we understand the human psyche itself to be an historical entity, subject to the vicissitudes of time and change, such truth cannot be timeless in an *a priori* sense. Any truth we discover in biblical history which still makes sense to us does so *a posteriori*, and is always subject to the possibility that it may become untrue with the further passage of time.

We shall take Ricoeur's version of the Oedipus hypothesis as the content of the surface meaning of the biblical father symbol, and use it as a means of access to the hidden meaning of the traditions. We shall follow the historical order of the traditions rather than making a systematic presentation; we shall not therefore give a precise analysis of the correlation between surface and deep meaning, but rather a running demonstration of how deeper aspects of the traditions are disclosed when the surface meaning of the symbol is kept in mind during the exposition.

---

30. See Excursus on Method, pp. 105–22.
31. Paul Ricoeur, *The Symbolism of Evil,* trans. Emerson Buchanan (Boston: Beacon, 1967).

CHAPTER 2

God the Father
in Jesus'
Religious Heritage

Jesus did not exist in a religious vacuum; he is the product of his ancestral Judaism, whose roots go back beyond Moses to the beginning of the second millennium B.C. and the legendary patriarchs Abraham, Isaac, and Jacob. One might expect, therefore, to find clear precedent in the Old Testament for the central importance of father as a divine symbol, since it is so predominant in the teaching of Jesus; but the evidence is surprisingly slender. There are only eleven places in the Old Testament where God is designated as "father,"[1] and none where he is explicitly invoked as such, while in the Gospels alone God is designated thus no less than one hundred and seventy times by Jesus, and never invoked by any other name in Jesus' prayers.[2] Even if we include the Old Testament passages where God's parenthood is implied,[3] the discrepancy between the Testaments is so great that we can only conclude that Jesus himself chose to give the symbol a special importance. In doing so he expressed his own peculiar experience of God, and this experience is what we are seeking to understand.

Jesus' emphasis on the father symbol was, to some extent, part of a trend in the Judaism of his time to increase its use, so the discontinuity between him and his tradition in the importance of the

---

1. Deut. 32:5; 2 Sam. 7:14; 1 Chron. 17:13; 22:10; 28:6; Ps. 89:26; Jer. 3:4–5; 31:9; Isa. 63:16; 64:8; Mal. 1:6. For an exhaustive presentation see the article by Gottfried Quell on "The Father Concept in the Old Testament" in the *Theological Dictionary of the New Testament* ed. G. Friedrich, trans. G. W. Bromiley (Grand Rapids: Eerdmans, 1967) V, 959–974 (cited TDNT hereafter).

2. Joachim Jeremias, "Abba" in *Abba, Studien zur neutestamentlichen Theologie und Zeitgeschichte* (Göttingen: Vandenhoeck und Ruprecht, 1966) 15–67, 33.

3. E.g. Exod. 4:22–23; Deut. 1:31; 8:5; Ps. 2:7; Jer. 3:19; 31:20; Hos. 11:1.

symbol is not as great as it seems at first sight; and even the discrepancy between him and the earlier Israelite theological traditions might be less than it seems, if we consider what we have chosen to call the "indirect symbolization" in which fatherhood is involved in these early sources.

The Bible believes that God acts in history. This means that there is a hidden dimension to historical experience that is aptly described in terms of creation and redemption. Yahweh is the proper name for this dimension, but its nature can only be understood by means of symbols. Ricoeur, interpreting von Rad, talks about "a network of signifying events" which generates a "surplus of meaning."[4] The significance or meaning of these events is precisely what the symbol makes available to thought. With reference to the father symbol, the Bible envisages two modes of relationship between it and this "surplus meaning," an indirect and a direct one. The former mode is symbolization by association while the latter is direct symbolization by metaphor or simile. In the indirect mode God is spoken of in connection with the human fathers; he is the "God of the fathers"; his association with the fathers is his chief identifying feature; when we want to think or speak of God we think and speak of the fathers. In the direct mode, the Bible uses either simile or metaphor: God is like a father, God is our father. We shall therefore divide our treatment of the Old Testament evidence into two parts, dealing first with the indirect and then with the direct symbolization.

INDIRECT SYMBOLIZATION

From the Father of the Gods to the
God of the Fathers[5]

The narratives in Genesis tell us that Israel's ancestors came from Ur of the Chaldees, by way of Harran (Gen. 11:31–32). The move to Harran, in northwestern Mesopotamia, may have been precipitated by the destruction of Ur in 1950 B.C. at the hands of the Elamites; but we cannot be sure. The narratives are sagas,

---

4. *The Conflict of Interpretations*, 46. For a discussion of this theme see our Excursus on Method, pp. 110–15.

5. For what follows we are indebted to E. O. James, *The Worship of the Sky God, A Comparative Study in Semitic and Indo-European Religion* (London: Athlone, 1963).

written after centuries of oral tradition, and therefore give a highly interpreted version of history. Nevertheless, archaeology and linguistic studies confirm the accuracy of their ethnological setting. From these sources we can confirm the biblical claim that Israel's ancestor was "a wandering Aramean" (Deut. 26:1), probably from a settlement on the plain of Aram—Padan-Aram, between Carchemish and Nineveh, where he "worshipped other gods" (Josh. 24:2). At the beginning of the second millennium B.C., the ancestors moved into Palestine, part of a larger migration of Arameans and Amorites, and settled in allied clans, to a semi-nomadic style of life. Approximately seven hundred years after the initial settlement (ca. 1200 B.C.), the tribes were more or less united through the agency of Moses, in the worship of the god Yahweh. Before Moses they worshipped gods that are recognizable as part of prevailing Canaanite religion, and it is with these gods of the pre-Mosaic ancestors that any consideration of the biblical understanding of God must begin.

The "other gods" which the fathers worshipped by the Euphrates were probably no different from those they worshipped when they entered Palestine—the divinities called in Canaanite "El," a conception of divinity which was common to all of western Asia at the time. According to the compilers of the traditions, writing after the Exodus and the settlement in the "promised land," Yahweh was "the God of the Fathers"; Abraham, however, would probably have considered "father of the gods" a more accurate description of his deity. For the god El, whom the fathers worshipped at various shrines, was the sky god, head of the Canaanite pantheon, whom the Ugaritic texts call "the father of gods and men," and describe in terms of generation and paternity, as the begetter of the world in a sexual sense rather than the creator,[6] who, as the later Yahweh, works by means of his Word alone, without any hint of sexuality. El is the west Semitic instance of the sky god, who as male and paternal, dominates the pantheons of the Semites and the Aryans.

Among the latter peoples he is initially, as in Sanskrit, Dyaus Pitar (= Zeus pater = Jupiter), the "father god," first clearly seen in the Rig Veda (1500–1000 B.C.). He was taken to India from his

---

6. *Ibid.,* 33.

place of origin on the eastern shores of the Caspian sea, by the light-skinned, Aryan-speaking Indo-Europeans who settled Sind and the Punjab between 1500 and 1200 B.C. Upon entering India the Aryans found, not a primitive culture, but the urban civilization of Harappa and Mohenjo-daro, whose chief divinity was probably the mother-goddess, as the many terra-cotta female figurines which have been excavated suggest.[7] Whether as a political compromise, or for reasons more integral to their theology, the Aryans portrayed Dyaus Pitar with a consort Prithivi, from whose union gods and men had their birth. They are respectively heaven (Dyaus = "the bright shining heavens") and earth, a correlation that is well known in Greek religion too, as Hesiod attests, where the creation of the world is the result of the coming together of the masculine "heaven" (*Ouranos*) and the feminine "earth" (*Gaia*).

The Semitic sky god can be traced back to a much earlier date than his Aryan cousin. He is found in the pantheon of the Sumerians, a people whose settlement in the valley of the Tigris and Euphrates began in the early fourth millennium B.C. Sumerian civilization was not Semitic; however, being composite it did contain Semitic elements (e.g. Semitic names in the list of the kings of Kish, 2800–2360 B.C.), and so the Semitic Akkadians who succeeded the Sumerians to prominence in 2350–2180 B.C. maintained a continuity of culture for Sumer and Akkad. The Sumerian pantheon was ruled by three deities, Anu, Enlil, and Ea. Anu was the sky god, Enlil the storm and wind god, and Ea the water god; each had his own shrine and city of patronage, respectively Uruk, Nippur, and Eridu. Each had a consort; Anu's original consort Antu was a colorless figure soon replaced by Inaana-Ishtar, the great mother, a move which could represent a political compromise with the goddess cult.[8] From the former union came only the underworld gods, the Anunnaki, and seven demons, the Asakki, while from the latter came the races of gods and men. Anu remained aloof, while Enlil was the agent of divine intervention in the world,[9] an early exam-

---

7. E. O. James, *The Cult of the Mother-Goddess, An Archaeological and Documentary Study* (London: Thames and Hudson, 1959).

8. See James, *Cult of the Mother-Goddess*; according to him the female "consorts" were originally the dominant divinities; the male was son-lover.

9. It is easy to see why the god of the storms should be conceived of as active, while the god of heaven, though supreme, was otiose.

ple of the tendency to replace the sky gods with more accessible, less transcendent deities. Thus, when Babylon was ascendent, Marduk, its tutelary divinity, became the active god, and when Assyria ruled, Ashur was most active. These younger active gods assume most of the power of the original three, without it being necessary to erase the originals from memory; they remain as a species of elder statesmen, with Anu as the primal father of the gods. The Canaanite counterpart to this theology is the relationship of El, the old, relatively otiose high god, and Aleyan Baal, the storm and fertility god, as we know from the Ugaritic texts (ca. mid-second millennium B.C.). El is the generic Canaanite word for "god," meaning "the powerful one." Specifically, although he occupies the same relative position as Anu, El is not identified with the sky. He dwells on "the mountain in the north," "at the sources of the (two) rivers, in the midst of the fountains of the two deeps,"[10] the mountain where the waters of the upper and lower firmament were thought to meet.

The compilers of the patriarchal sagas in Genesis believed that the fathers worshipped El: as El Elyon (= God most high, 14:18–24), El Olam (= the everlasting God, 21:33), El Roi (= God of a vision, 16:13), El Shaddai (= God almighty, 17:1; 43:14), El Bethel (= the God of the place, Bethel, 31:13; 35:7). These compound names show that such worship took place through some other deity. The clearest example is the name El Shaddai, where Shaddai means "the mountain one,"[11] who is in a filial relationship to El. El Elyon may refer to the relationship between El and the Aleyan Baal (a storm god). El Bethel shows that the god was also associated with a place and worshipped through that relationship (28:10–22). Thus we have the high god El, worshipped through lower, more active gods, associated sometimes with special places—the mountain, Bethel—and sometimes with special experiences—of power, a vision, the passing of time, the heights of heaven. Accordingly, there is no firm basis for the conjecture that the patriarchs held a monotheistic theology, worshipping only the high God. The fathers venerated the gods of various sacred places, as Abraham's association with Shechem and the terebinth tree at Moreh shows (Gen. 12:6–7).

10. James, *Sky God*, 32.
11. *Ibid.*, 48.

Bethel, Beersheba, Hebron, Mamre and Ophrah were also such "places related to the god."

Nevertheless, although we cannot find a monotheism among the patriarchs, there was a movement towards it at this early stage. We may assume that these originally distinct gods were associated together at some stage of the tradition, by being identified as manifestations of the one high god, El. There is no reason to assume that this linking together of the various gods through El could not have been made by the Israelite ancestors. As James remarks, "unless there had been some confederation of the Hebrew tribes on a theocratic basis before the Exodus, the attitude, position and achievement of Moses are inexplicable."[12] This is a reasonable assumption, and the evidence suggests that the theocratic element in this early confederation took the form of a general veneration of El, the father of the gods, in terms of whom the individual godlings of the fathers were associated with one another. The godlings were not erased from theology, neither were they necessarily identified with one another; rather the otiose high god El provided a principle of unity, became the one expressed in the many, without making the many one. So while we cannot speak of a pre-Mosaic "El-Monotheism," we can nevertheless point to a supreme god who is the source and origin of all things, the father of gods and humanity. Herein lay one point of contact with later Yahwistic monotheism.

Another point of contact between pre-Mosaic and Mosaic theology may be found in the hints that each of the great patriarchs had a god associated with himself: the "El of Abraham," the "Fear of Isaac" (Gen. 31:42, 53) and the "Strong One of Jacob" (49:24–25). In this latter text we have a series of striking synonyms: "the Strong one of Jacob" = "the Rock (Shepherd) of Israel" = "the God of your father" = "El Shaddai." In the first two texts the designations are also synonymous with "the God of my father." "If the God of my father, the God of Abraham and the Fear of Isaac, had not been with me, you would have sent me away empty handed" (31:42). The "El" of Abraham might well have been the high god, father of gods and men; the name Abraham means "the father is exalted"[13]

12. *Ibid.*, 49.

13. E. A. Speiser, *Genesis, The Anchor Bible* (Garden City: Doubleday, 1964) 124, n. 5.

and this could refer to the divinity. It appears that the tradition in these texts knew of these special patriarchal gods and their more general designation "the god of my father," as well as their identification with El. Thus we have our second point of contact with later Yahwism, the concept of the god of the fathers.

A third such common feature—really implied in the second—is that the god is identified by his relationship to a person, rather than to a place or to natural phenomena such as the sun or storms or fertility. Such a relationship is not entirely unprecedented in the ancient Near East; Enlil was committed to his city Nippur, Marduk to Babylon, and Ashur to Nineveh, and we may assume that this commitment was channelled through the king. Likewise, in the designation "the god of my father" is implied the relationship of the god to the whole tribe, of which the father is the representative and ancestor. Certainly, the traditions we have considered suggest that the relationship between the god and the father extends to his descendants. The differentiating feature in this Israelite theology is that the god is pledged to a semi-nomad, and so the element of place is relatively unimportant, compared to the case of Marduk and Babylon. The element of personal commitment is, however, commensurately stronger, and the symbol of the god's nature and presence is the person of the average father, rather than a graven image or a sacred place.

This is an important development for our interest. With the shift from place to person in the symbolization of the divine we get the first clear indication of the fact that the locus of God's revelation is to be the realm of human relations and human actions, called history. More specifically, it is to be the realm of the family. Thus the family becomes the locus of divine manifestation, and the father its symbolic focus.[14] From this association between God and the father comes the impulse for such excessive veneration as is expressed in the Noah story, where Ham is cursed for merely looking on his father's nakedness (Gen. 9:20–25), and in the decalogue, where the command to honor parents occurs in association with the commandments about our duties to God (1–4) rather than with those to our fellow human beings (6–10; Exod. 20:12). It is a

14. Cf. Quell, "Father," *TDNT* V, 966–9.

species of the veneration of the ancestors, well known in African religion and in Confucianism: the ancestors are, however, not worshipped themselves, but the worship of God takes place in conjunction with the ancestors, by remembering them and using that memory to identify the god.

The earliest traces of theology in the Bible, therefore, outline a god who is known through a personal relationship which, in turn, is re-presented by remembering the ancestors; and who also has vague elements of universality in his nature. He is the begetter of gods and humanity in his Canaanite form, although this is never expressed in the biblical traditions. He is the high god and he is the near god, involved in the lives of the families and tribes. He is the transcendent originator who determines all things, and the immanent companion who arranges everything. The symbol of his being and presence is the father of the family, who, in turn, is responsible for that family's worship and obedience to God. To share in God's blessing one had to belong to a family. Thus the status of the father was divinely sanctioned and the divine was involved in the history of the individual and society at the most intimate level, the level of the family.

This is not to say that the influence of the symbol "father" was all one way, from the earthly father to God. Rather, we recognize an interaction between the theological tradition—the God idea defined "from above"—and family experience—the God idea defined "from below." From the history of the god concept we learn that earthly fatherhood was seen as the source of life and the guarantor of order in the family, and from the history of fatherhood in Israel we learn that God was associated with the experience of sustenance and education.[15] It is not surprising that imagery "from below" should be drawn from experience in the family, for the family was the basic unit of society and the father the head of the family. Although the evidence comes from the later Yahwistic level of the tradition, we may assume that the accounts that earliest Israel was organized on a patrilineal principle, into families, tribes, and clans

---

15. P. A. H. de Boer, *Fatherhood and Motherhood in Israelite and Judean Piety* (Leiden: Brill, 1974) ; Quell, "Father," 966–9; M. Juritsch, *Der Vater in Familie und Welt* (Paderborn: Schöningh, 1966) 113, mentions that surveys show the role of educator still to be characteristic of paternal self-understanding.

(Josh. 7; 1 Sam. 10:17–26) reflect a circumstance that goes back to the time of the patriarchs. From the beginning an Israelite experienced life as family life, and it is not surprising that the symbols for the experience of God should be drawn from this context.

The evidence for this archaic stage in the history of the biblical concept of God is too slender to draw any more than these rather general conclusions; nevertheless the fundamental relationship between God and the father figure is established, and something of the significance of this relationship has been explored.

From the God of the Fathers to the God of Moses

Between the thirteenth and the tenth centuries B.C., a decisive development took place in the theology of Israel. Under the guidance of Moses, a prophet, lawgiver, and leader of inspired proportions, the Israelite tribes were united in allegiance to the god Yahweh. The work of those influenced by Moses can be detected wherever the name Yahweh is used for God in the books of Genesis through Numbers. The northern Israelite document in Exodus called "Elohist" uses the name "Elohim" for the god of Moses, possibly maintaining thereby a closer connection with the pre-Mosaic god. In any case, the name Yahweh predominates in the Pentateuch and subsequent sources, and the Yahwistic theologians who present the Mosaic theology most consistently put their theological stamp on the concept of God for all subsequent traditions.

The Yahwists also interpreted previous theology in the light of their presuppositions, not least of which was that Yahweh manifests himself in history. Consonant with this conviction, Yahwistic theology presents revelation in the form of narrative. Accordingly they arranged the pre-Mosaic traditions—oral and written, more or less connected—into a continuous narrative of the origins of Israel, from the creation of the world to the slavery in Egypt, which is the immediate backdrop for Moses. The patriarchs Abraham, Isaac, and Jacob may originally have been separate tribal ancestors who in the course of time became associated with one another as their tribes and clans were allied. We have seen it probable that some such progress toward unification of societies and theology had taken place before the advent of the Yahwists, and that the idea of a high god who is involved in the history of persons and society was already present. To this inchoate theology the Yahwists brought clarity and definition, organizing the diverse strands into what we now know as the patriarchal narratives of Genesis with the God of Moses, Yahweh, as the one deity worshipped by all the fathers.

Yahweh's identity is bound up with "the fathers." The account of the revelation of the Name in Exodus 3 includes all the essential elements of the Yahwists' theology and demonstrates how "the fathers" are used to identify Yahweh. Moses, while tending the flock of his father-in-law in Midian, comes to Horeb, "the mountain of God." On the slopes of the sacred mountain he has a vision of a burning bush, which burns but is not consumed. As he draws near, Yahweh calls to him from the midst of the flames,

> "Moses, Moses" . . . "I am the God of your forefathers, the God of Abraham, the God of Isaac, the God of Jacob . . . I have indeed seen the misery of my people in Egypt . . . I have taken heed of their sufferings, and have come down to rescue them from the power of Egypt, and to bring them out of that country into a fine broad land . . . I will send you to Pharaoh and you shall bring my people Israel out of Egypt . . . 'I am'; that is who I am. Tell them that 'I am' has sent you to them . . . You must tell the Israelites this, that it is YHWH [Yahweh] the God of their forefathers, the God of Abraham, the God of Isaac and the God of Jacob who has sent you to them. This is my name for ever; this is my title in every generation" (Exod. 3:1–15; NEB adapted).

The elements in this passage, which are also the fundamental themes of Yahwism, may be summarized as follows: (i) the call of Moses; (ii) the self-identification of Yahweh as the same God who was known by the fathers; (iii) the (promised) self-revelation of God in delivering his own people from slavery and granting them a land to dwell in, entailing the notion of God's acting in history and his commitment to his own people (election and promise); (iv) the commissioning of Moses to be the instrument of God's saving act, entailing the notion that God acts in history through chosen individuals; (v) the revelation of the name Yahweh—which could be interpreted to mean "the source of all there is," "the one who causes history to happen" or an ironic refusal to give a name (ultimately the name conceals as much as it reveals, as our inability to pinpoint the meaning attests); (vi) the repetition, in emphatic terms, that Yahweh is the same God as the God of the fathers.

Thus we have four identifying marks for Yahweh: Moses; the fathers; the mighty deeds in the Exodus and the promise of the land; the name Yahweh. Each determines the meaning of the other; they are to be interpreted together; and indeed, they frequently occur together in the traditions. ("Yahweh, the God of the fathers and of Moses who brought us out of Egypt and promised us the land.")[16]

The Yahwists arranged the pre-Mosaic traditions in narrative sequence (= revelation in history) and presented the role of the fathers commensurately with their importance in the revelation of Yahweh. There is a certain correspondence between Moses and the fathers: just as Moses is called, commissioned, and promised, so is Abraham (Gen. 12:1–3)—the fundamental promise to Abraham is of a land and descendants (Genesis 15), a promise which the P source (Genesis 17) elaborates by means of the change of name, so that Abraham is called "the father of many nations" (Gen. 17:5). The promise to Moses is also a promise of deliverance and a land. More important for our purposes, however, than this correspondence are the differences between the Mosaic stage and "the fathers."

The close relation between God and the fathers in the patriarchal stage of theology suggests that the only way to be related to God is by membership in the family of the fathers, by natural descent. The father's blessing, passed on to his eldest son, is a major part of the ancient concept of paternity, as the drama of Isaac, Jacob, and Esau testifies (Genesis 27 and 28). In Genesis 27 and 28 Jacob receives his father's blessing, albeit by treachery (unlike Moses in Exodus 3), lives his life in the power of this blessing, and presumably passes it on to his descendants. Isaac's natural descendants, therefore, are the only beneficiaries of the blessing; their salvation depends on their staying at home.

The Yahwists' presentation of the God-relationship and the way to experience God's blessing in Gen. 12:1–3 changes this old patriarchal notion decisively by insisting that fellowship with

16. E.g. Exod. 20:1; Deut. 26:5–9; Josh. 24:2–13.

Yahweh entails leaving the house of one's fathers (12:1). The history of salvation begins with Abraham's willingness to leave home, to break kinship ties. This demand is most vividly presented in Exod. 32:29, where the Levites are accepted as especially dedicated to Yahweh because they turned against their own sons and brothers, slaughtering them for betraying Yahweh with the golden calf.

> Today you have consecrated yourselves to the Lord completely, because you have turned each against his own son and his own brother and so have this day brought a blessing upon yourselves.

As in Gen. 12:1-3, the blessing is given to those who break the ties of family. This is probably the point of the strange story of the attempted sacrifice of Isaac in Genesis 22. Abraham had to break the paternal ties in order for the relationship between him and Isaac to be by election alone.

The phenomenon we are witnessing is well described as election. Its paradigm is the call of Moses in Exodus 3 which we have just examined. Yahweh chooses someone for a task and pledges his own blessing to the chosen one. As Yahweh has freely chosen him or her so the elect has to respond freely and responsibly. Thus the idea of election profoundly reformulates the idea of fatherhood. The unprecedented act of leaving one's father's house, where one's blessing resides, of stepping outside of the sacred circle of the family, leaving behind the graves of the ancestors, becomes the paradigm of the relationship to God. The unnatural act of turning against one's sons and siblings becomes the model of faith, which trusts the invisible God to bless one, in his own mysterious way. It is a breaking of the familial ties of patriarchy, a rending of the order of nature for the sake of opening oneself to the experience of grace.

This reformulation probably took place when the symbolization began to shift from the indirect mode of Yahweh as the God of the fathers to Yahweh as God the Father. Mosaic theology wanted to eradicate any hint of the mythological idea that God is the actual progenitor of his people, a notion that clung to the person of the high god El whom the patriarchs worshipped in the manner we have seen. Sexuality is to be emphatically excluded from the idea of God. In order to express this new and characteristically Mosaic theology, the Yahwists chose the image of adoption.[17] The relationship between God and his people is that of father and *adopted* son:

> I am Yahweh, I will release you from your labours in Egypt . . . I will adopt you as my people, and I will become your God . . . I will lead you to the land which I swore with uplifted hand to give to Abraham, to Isaac, to Jacob . . . (Exod. 6:6–8).

In this sense we should also understand Exod. 4:22–23, part of the mysterious recapitulation of Moses' call in 4:19–26:

> Israel is my first-born son. I have told you to let my son go, so that he may worship me. You have refused to let him go, so I will kill your first-born son (4:23).

Thus the hint of God as father-progenitor which derives from El, "the father of gods and men," is expunged by means of the notion of adoption, or, in later theological language, "election."

Election describes a relationship based on free choice without reference to the bonds of kinship. In our literature it is formalized in a covenant between God and the fathers (Genesis 15 and 17) and God and the nation (Exodus 19). God and his people enter into an agreement; there is no 'natural' and ineluctable bond between them. The bonds of kinship (mythological) are severed, and the relationship is restored on the level of free and responsible choice. So we have our first example of the Oedipal structure of the symbolization. The bonds of fate are broken and a new relationship established, beyond God the natural father.

This insight is corroborated in one of the more puzzling features of the patriarchal narratives, namely the repeated threats to the wife's virtue. Twice Abraham exposes Sarah, and Isaac jeopardizes Rebecca's virtue once (Genesis 12, 20, and 26). At first sight these accounts underline the importance of the wife's role in election. She is essential to the future of the blessing because from her alone can its next bearer be born. In 17:19 ff. God declares that he will fulfil his purpose through Isaac (yet to be born) and not through the already present Ishmael; through the son born to Abraham's wife, not through the son of the slave girl. It is important that the bearer of the blessing have the right mother as well as the right father; father and mother together are the bearers and conveyors

17. Jeremias, *Abba*, 17.

of the blessing. That is why the wives—Sarah, Rebecca, and Rachel —are so prominent in the narratives. It was Rebecca who "made" Jacob, and in the charming account of the first meeting between Isaac and Rebecca we catch a glimpse of what Sarah meant to her son: "Isaac conducted her into the tent of Sarah his mother and took her as his wife. So she became his wife, and he loved her and was consoled for the death of his mother" (24:67). If ever a statement suggested the need to loosen the bonds of kinship, the need to resolve an Oedipal relationship, it is this one;[18] but there is more to these texts than random Freudian elements.

We suggest that the accounts of Sarah's and Rebecca's abandonment to the harems of strangers, their being presented as sister rather than wife, is a device for loosening the kinship bonds, and substituting the bonds of election and grace. Not even the natural relationships between husband and wife are adequate to symbolize God's activity. By all reasonable expectations the two mothers of the promise should have become the wives of strangers (because of their husbands' cowardice). By the direct intervention of God's grace they are preserved and restored to their undeserving husbands. As a result they appear, like Isaac after the attempted sacrifice, as "returned from the dead," with an independence and freedom in their renewed commitment. Theirs is a relationship of a new covenant. In addition to the theme of the jeopardized wife, further evidence for our interpretation occurs in the motif of the lost son. The Jacob saga continues the account of the jeopardized wife, when Leah is substituted for Rachel, and Rachel is barren (29–30), but the important part of the Jacob saga for our purposes is the story of Joseph, the son who became the instrument of God's election by being cut off from his family, through sibling rivalry. Such a severing of the ties of kinship was necessary before Joseph could become "a father [= counselor] to Pharaoh" (45:8) and the instrument of salvation for the world, in the short run through providing for the world during the famine, and in the long run by providing the necessary background for the Exodus and Sinai, and thus for Yahweh's revelation to the world through Moses.

18. Cf. Theodor Reik, "Unbewusste Faktoren in der wissenschaftlichen Bibelarbeit," in *Psychoanalytische Interpretationen biblischer Texte,* ed. Yorick Spiegel (Munich: Kaiser, 1972) 358–63.

Thus the theme of the severance of family ties is well attested. It can be interpreted within the terms of "theology as usual" to signify the priority of the covenant with God before all other covenants, the initiative of grace and its transforming power. When, however, we enquire more closely about the effects of this transforming power we must take account of the fact that they are described in terms of family relationships. A relationship—between father and son, wife and husband, mother and son, brother and brother—is broken, and then it is restored at a new level, a level which in the traditions is the level of grace. It is surely not fortuitous that this rhythm corresponds to Ricoeur's exposition of the three stages in the Oedipal experience of every human being: the Oedipus complex (= the initial kinship); the negotiation of the complex (= a breaking of the kinship bond); the persistence of the complex (= the restoration of the relationship on a level of mutual recognition). Whatever else these Mosaic traditions are saying, this word is also spoken: salvation is a new relationship of mutual trust and recognition with the significant others in one's life, a relationship that enables one to enter the larger arena of life as liberated (= to participate in the Exodus) and to remember one's fathers with hope (= to believe the promise of a good future).

The Fathers as a Symbol of Saving History

The covenant with the fathers included God's promise of descendants and a good land. Until the seventh century the promise to the fathers was one among several concepts by which Yahweh was identified, of more or less equal importance with the others. We considered four in the previous section: the association with Moses, the association with the fathers, the declaration of the Exodus and the promise of the land, and the name Yahweh. In the seventh century, as Deuteronomy attests, the promise of the land to the fathers assumes greater significance than before. This is probably because the Deuteronomists wrote in the light of the fall of the kingdom of Assyria and Judah's hope of regaining the Northern Kingdom which was colonized by Assyria in 722 B.C. By emphasizing the promise of the land to the fathers they asserted their right to possession.

With Deuteronomy in the seventh century we are in the midst of the period of prophecy, a time when the father symbol came to be used directly. The starting point for consideration of the present theme lies, therefore, in the eighth century prophet Hosea. In Hos. 9:10, "I came upon Israel like grapes in the wilderness, I looked on their forefathers with joy like the first ripe figs," we encounter an "old" idea[19] also found in Deut. 32:8, namely, that Yahweh "found" Israel in the wilderness. This obviously serves the theme of adoption over against procreation by the god, a motif we have already met in the Yahwistic tradition. Yahweh "adopted" a foundling; and Hos. 9:10 emphasizes the joy with which he did so. To be a father of Israel is to be "found" by God ("I looked on their forefathers with joy"); fatherhood is constituted, therefore, by the experience of God's election; it is the channel through which God's grace comes to us, the sign of God's nature and presence.

Furthermore, as the image of being "found" suggests, the moment of their adoption (election) is the moment of their coming into being as a people. "Father" is the symbol for the reception of life, and so "father" here functions more like "mother" in the sense that it symbolizes the reception rather than the initiation of life. This maternal element in the symbolization is confirmed by the following verses, where God threatens a judgment that will mean "no child-birth, no fruitful womb, no conceiving" (vv. 11 and 12) and further when the prophet cries, "Give them a womb that miscarries and dry breasts" (v. 14), and God warns, "If ever they give birth I will slay the dearest offspring of their womb" (v. 16). This horrible warning is cast in terms of the over-arching metaphor of Israel as an unfaithful wife.[20] Thus, the ancestors as symbols of the people's experience of God's blessing, of God's gracious election, can be thought of as either fathers or mothers. The "ancestors" are symbols of God's grace, of the history of salvation, mothers and fathers together.

This joyful reference to the "fathers" occurs in the midst of an indictment, as a foil to Israel's sin. Yahweh's act of adoption, symbolized by the fathers, has been forgotten by a people who are unfaithful. Unfaithfulness and forgetfulness go together; repentance and remembrance go together—the remembrance of God's promise to the fathers. This conjunction of the father figure and indictment

19. G. von Rad, *Deuteronomy, A Commentary* (London: 1966) re 32:8.
20. The section begins in 9:1 with "like a wanton you have forsaken your God."

is a relatively constant element in the texts, as we shall see in due course, constant enough to demand an explanation. Our introduction to the prophetic stage of the tradition, therefore, gives us three guiding motifs: father as a symbol of adoption (election); father functioning like mother in the symbolization and suggesting a fluidity between the two parental figures; and father-mother as a foil to the people's sinfulness, a ground for indictment.

Central to the prophetic tradition is the book of Deuteronomy, and the Deuteronomic history which includes the books of Joshua, Judges, Samuel, and Kings. We enter the Deuteronomic tradition through the portal of the so-called "covenant renewal" record in Joshua 24. In a characteristically Deuteronomic speech Joshua identifies the addressees with the "fathers."

> I brought *your fathers* out of Egypt and *you* came to the Red Sea. The Egyptians sent their chariots and cavalry to pursue *your fathers* to the sea. But when they appealed to the Lord, he put a screen of darkness between *you* and the Egyptians, and brought the sea down on them and it covered them; *you* saw for yourselves what I did to Egypt (vv. 6–7).

The "fathers" are traced all the way back to Terah and his sons Abraham and Nahor, who worshipped other gods beside the Euphrates, and who made the decision to follow Yahweh. Joshua tells the whole of the history of God's saving acts from that initial call to the settlement of the land, as if his hearers were participants in the experiences of the "fathers." Indeed, the decision he calls them to make "this day" is a repetition of the decision which the fathers made beside the Euphrates and upon entering the land, to worship Yahweh rather than the gods of those places.

Joshua 24 might reflect the memory of a covenant renewal festival in ancient Israel, or it might be a piece of Deuteronomic artifice. In any case, we know from Deut. 26:5–10 that a credo of God's gracious deeds for and with the fathers was at the center of Israelite religious self-consciousness at a very early stage.[21] Von Rad believes that some such credo was the wellspring of the historical traditions in the Old Testament; and although this theory has become uncer-

---

21. Gerhard von Rad, *Old Testament Theology*, vol. 1, *The Theology of Israel's Historical Traditions*, trans. D. M. G. Stalker (New York: Harper and Row, 1962) 121 ff.

tain in more recent scholarship, the existence of early credos which contain the significant experiences of the fathers, with which the descendants identify, is assured. Deut. 26:5 begins: "My father was a homeless Aramean who went down to Egypt with a small company"; then after reciting the oppression, it continues, *"We* cried to the Lord [Yahweh] the God of our fathers for help, and he listened to us . . . and . . . brought us out of Egypt . . . to this place and gave us this land, a land flowing with milk and honey" (vv. 7–9). According to Deuteronomy, this confession was to be made at the presentation of the offering of the firstfruits, as a recognition that the possession of the land which gives such fruits is the result of Yahweh's grace to the fathers, and to their descendants. Relationship with God depends, therefore, on identifying with the fathers in their experience of God's electing grace. In the event of the Exodus, God adopted the fathers and all those who freely identify themselves with the fathers. "The fathers" are a symbol for the possibility of the present experience of electing grace.

The land was the special gift to the fathers, and present possession of it was secured by the memory that God had sworn the land on oath to the fathers. Deut. 1:8 introduces a recurring refrain in Deuteronomy: "I have laid the land open before you; go in and occupy it, *the land which the Lord swore to give to your forefathers Abraham, Isaac and Jacob,* and to their descendants after them" (6:18–19; 8:1; 9:5; 10:11; 11:9; 26:3; 28:11; 30:20; 34:4; cf. Exod. 13:5, 11; Num. 14:16, 23, 30). Not only the possession of the land, but the whole work of salvation which made possession possible was based on the oath to the fathers:

> It was not because you were more numerous than any other nation that the Lord cared for you and chose you, for you were the smallest of all nations; it was because the Lord loved you and stood by his oath to your forefathers, that he brought you out with his strong hand and redeemed you from the land of slavery (Deut. 7:7–8; cf. 9:5) .

Thus memory secures the present and is the ground for good hope: "The Lord your God is a merciful god: he will never fail you nor destroy you, nor will he forget the covenant guaranteed by oath with your forefathers" (4:31). The memory of God's saving acts, the history of salvation, is a memory of the experience of the fathers, and their descendants identify themselves with the fathers as the objects of this beneficial activity. God's oath to the fathers is God's oath to us.[22]

In Deuteronomic circles this identification meant salvation; the fathers were symbols of salvation in history. In Freud identification with the father is at first an expression of the desire to be like the father, which subsequently becomes the drive to replace the father in the mother's affections. In these biblical traditions we have an identification beyond the pathological stages of the Oedipus situation, in which the same energy, which at the earlier stages would be vicious, is life-giving and healing—the energy of a good memory and a good hope. Once again it seems as if the Oedipal complex has been negotiated in the way Ricoeur describes as optimal.

DIRECT SYMBOLIZATION

It is now time to complete the transition from indirect to direct symbolization, which we have seen to be going on ever since the advent of Moses, and to consider the father (mother) as a simile or metaphor for God. We place "mother" in parentheses because, while the symbolization does not exclude her, it only implies her presence. It will be part of our endeavor to make this implication explicit.

Father (Mother) as a Symbol for God

The first texts we shall consider as we move on to direct symbolization, are those in which it is implied rather than explicitly stated that God is a father to his people. In Hosea 9 we saw how the human forefathers (mothers) symbolize the experience of God's electing (adopting) grace, and function as a foil to God's indictment of Israel's sin. In the texts we shall consider now, the fathers are more than merely a sign of God's nature and presence; now God himself is father. We have moved from symbolization by association to direct symbolization by metaphor and simile.

In the midst of an indictment of Israel for cowardice before the power of the inhabitants they had to oust from the promised land, the following occurs: "You saw there (in Egypt and in the wilderness) how the Lord your God carried you all the way to this place, as a father carries his son" (Deut. 1:31); and in the wilderness wan-

---

22. Such identification occurred not only in Deuteronomic circles, but throughout the subsequent history of biblical faith, as 1 Cor. 10:1 ff. attests.

dering, "the Lord your God was disciplining you as a father disciplines his son" (Deut. 8:5; cf. Ps. 103:13). The idea that Israel was God's son is well attested,[23] and this sonship is usually associated with the wilderness period. Hosea 11 is a classic statement of this idea:

> When Israel was a boy, I loved him; I called my son out of Egypt . . . It was I who taught Ephraim to walk, I who had taken them in my arms, but they did not know that I harnessed them in leading-strings and led them with bonds of love, that I had lifted them like a little child to my cheek, that I had bent down to feed them (Hos. 11:1–4; cf. 10) .

Clearly, therefore, in some prophetic circles and among the Deuteronomists the Exodus was understood as an experience of Yahweh's parenthood, which, up to the present has usually been described as God's "fatherhood."

Fatherhood may, however, be too narrow a designation. In Hos. 11:4 Yahweh is said to have "bent down to feed them," a function performed by the mother; and in a Deuteronomic passage in Numbers 11 Moses implies that God is Israel's mother who brought him to birth and must carry him in her bosom.

> How have I displeased the Lord that I am burdened with the care of this whole people? Am I their mother? Have I brought them into the world, and am I called upon to carry them in my bosom, like a nurse with her babies, to the land promised by thee on oath to their fathers? (Num. 11:11–12) .

Moses is not their mother who gave them birth and is therefore responsible for nursing them; God is!

Ricoeur says that in Hosea 11 the symbol is mixed, beginning with father in v. 1 and ending with mother in v. 4. This view is based on a reading of v. 1 in the light of an idea like that expressed in Deut. 1:31. On the face of it, however, Hos. 11:1–4 speaks of God as mother—there is no "mixing." In the Numbers passage (11:11–12) there is an *ad hoc* (*ad divinitatem?*) atmosphere surrounding the expostulation of Moses, so we cannot put too much weight on it as

---

23. E.g. Exod. 4:22b–23; Jer. 31:9; Deut. 1:31; B. Gerhardsson, *The Testing of God's Son (Matt. 4:1–11 and par.), An Analysis of an Early Christian Midrash,* Coniectanea Biblica; New Testament Series 2 (Lund: C. W. K. Gleerup, 1966) 20–24.

evidence of an established symbolization of God as mother. On the other hand, it could be maintained that the father symbol is not established either, and has an element of the *ad hoc* about it too. In any case, God is Israel's mother in these two passages.

There are other examples of this image: in Isa. 49:15, Yahweh's care for Israel is compared to a mother's care for her child—"Can a woman forget the infant at her breast, or a loving mother the child of her womb? Even these forget, yet will I not forget you." In Isa. 66:10–13 we find a designation of God as mother, like those for father in Deut. 1:31 and 8:5. The Lord promises to bless Jerusalem so that her people may "suck and be fed from the breasts that give comfort . . ."; the blessing "shall suckle you, and you shall be carried in their arms and dandled on their knees. As a mother comforts her son, so will I myself comfort you. . . ." The restored Jerusalem is the mother of her people; ultimately, however, their mother is God who restores Jerusalem and makes her able to nourish her children. It would seem, then, that at one level the direct symbolization presents God as both father and mother of the people.

The background of this parent imagery may be the Canaanite worship of father and mother divinities, attested in a text like Jer. 2:27: ". . . they say, 'You are our father' to a block of wood and cry 'Mother' to a stone. . . ." The Yahwistic theologians claim for Yahweh the functions of the other gods and therefore present him as father and mother together, since the two roles which polytheism assigns to two separate figures respectively are combined in one monotheistic god. Deut. 32:18 expresses this dual nature of Yahweh, as father and mother, in one sentence: "You forsook the rock who begot you [father], and the God who gave you birth [mother]" (cf. Jer. 16:3).[24] There is a more general background, however, than the Canaanite religion, in the family structure of ancient Israel.

We have seen how Israel was a patriarchal society organized into families, tribes, and clans according to patrilineal relationships. A family was called "the house of the father" (*bet 'ab*) and usually comprised three generations. It was essential to be buried with the fathers to remain within the sphere of the family blessing. The fam-

24. De Boer, *Fatherhood*, 42.

ily was also the center of cultic life (1 Samuel 1).[25] The status of a wife within the family is the subject of debate in current scholarship. The received opinion is that it was very low: the husband was her master (*ba 'al*) and lord (*'adōn*) and she belonged in the same category as his slaves and animals (Exod. 20:17). Adultery by a woman was essentially a violation of a man's property rights, and marital fidelity was an obligation not shared by the man.[26] This situation was merely a manifestation of the general depreciation of female worth, vividly expressed in Lev. 27:1 ff. where a female is assessed at three-fifths the value of a male. But the received opinion may be too dire, as John Otwell has argued,[27] and as seems probable based on the fact that the prophetic traditions symbolize God not as father alone, but as father and mother.

As Otwell suggests, much depends on one's point of departure in assessing the evidence. If one assumes a woman-oppressing patriarchy one will find evidence to prove it; if one assumes a more balanced relationship between the sexes, the same evidence can be read to prove that.[28] We find support for the latter assumption in the father/mother symbolization used by the prophets. To be sure, one cannot portray the biblical family as a partnership between husband and wife, but it is true, in Otwell's words, that

> we have been forced by this point of departure to magnify the status of women, to see the role of the male as essentially complementary and supportive, and to provide an explanation of the evidence describing the relationships between the sexes which is an alternative to a now untenable traditional paternalistic view.[29]

Here is a sample of Otwell's argumentation: wives are not ranked with slaves and chattels in Exod. 20:17, but rather mentioned as the first and most important person in the household;[30] it is a sign of their status that in the Old Testament women name children twenty-

---

25. *Ibid.*
26. F. Hauck, "Moicheuo," *TDNT,* IV, 730: "Hence a man is not under obligation to avoid all non-marital intercourse. Unconditional fidelity is demanded only of the woman, who in marriage becomes the possession of her husband."
27. *And Sarah Laughed.*
28. *Ibid.,* 86.
29. *Ibid.,* 87.
30. *Ibid.,* 76.

five times while men do so only twenty times;[31] women are able to divorce their husbands (Exod. 21:10);[32] the longer period of purification of the mother required after the birth of a daughter than of a son (Lev. 12:2–5) shows that more 'holiness' attaches to such a birth, since ritual contamination was essentially a being charged with the substance of the divine.[33] In sum, the fecundity of women was regarded as "the most crucial and clearest proof of God's presence in the midst of his people."[34]

Like all pioneers, Otwell may have gone too far; he almost persuades us that the reverse of the traditional paternalistic view is the case, and that women are the chief agents of God's purpose. We would settle for a view that makes the father/mother symbolization of God credible, and for that purpose it is enough to demonstrate a reasonable mutuality in the marriage relationship. Furthermore, the symbolization is constructed from the point of view of a child, to whom parents may appear in a harmonious relationship, equally worthy of honor (Exod. 20:12); but the sociologically minded observer sees inequities not apparent to the child.

The overall impression of family life in the Bible is a positive one, especially by comparison with contemporaneous Greek sources. Sibling rivalry is relatively prominent in the early biblical narratives, and the house of David had its share of strife, but there is nothing in the Bible to compare with the cycles of internecine slaughter involving wives, husbands, and children which the Greek tragic tradition contains. If we accept Philip Slater's thesis[35] that the Greek myths tell us about relations in the society which produced them, and extend it, *mutatis mutandis,* to cover the biblical narratives, we might conclude that relationships in the latter patriarchal families were better than in the former. The reason for this, according to Slater,[36] is that in the biblical families the patriarch was a present father, while in Greece he was absent.

31. *Ibid.,* 112.
32. *Ibid.,* 121. If a concubine has these rights, *a fortiori* so does a wife.
33. *Ibid.,* 176-7.
34. *Ibid.,* 61.
35. *The Glory of Hera, Greek Mythology and the Greek Family* (Boston: Beacon, 1968).
36. *Ibid.,* 334-5.

In other words, the maternal threat in the biblical family was cush-
ioned by the provision of a strong male role model, while in Greece it
was not, producing a more brittle, phallic, and narcissistic male, long-
ing for a father but unable to tolerate one.[37]

In Greece the fathers absented themselves from the family, congre-
gating in homosexual brotherhoods. Thus the mothers were left to
put the sons in place of the fathers whom they hated; and a son thus
treated, to a mixed-message of love and hate, becomes narcissistic
(i.e. "to have a deep concern and doubt about the integrity and
value—not in moral terms but in something closer to a monetary
sense—of the self")[38] and "highly Oedipal" (i.e. "to be oriented toward an unattainable goal, to be trapped in fantasy, alienated from
experience . . . to be competitive, dissatisfied, grandiose").[39] The situation was a vicious circle because the absence of the fathers produced sons who would in turn remove themselves from their families: "A society which derogates women produces envious mothers
who produce narcissistic males who are prone to derogate women."[40]
It is an argument from silence, but the contrast between the Bible
and the Greeks in this regard is so striking that we might safely infer
that whatever difficulties the ancient Israelite family may have had,
those caused by the absence of the father were not chief among them.

Father was a positive figure in their psycho-social experience. The
relationship between the father and the mother does not seem to
have been perceived by the children as one of conflict, nor, indeed,
were their roles sharply distinguished. Indeed, father and mother
could be a single unit of meaning (Jer. 16:3; Judg. 14:2). The ease
with which the prophetic symbolizers move between the designations "father" and "mother" suggests that the combined role of
parent was not solely based on the exigencies of monotheism when
faced with the need to represent what was formerly presented by two
polytheistic godlings. It also rested on the experience of the good
parent in an Israelite family.

Nevertheless, the society was patriarchal and the prerogatives of
patriarchy, some of the less humane of which we have already

37. *Ibid.*
38. *Ibid.*, 454.
39. *Ibid.*, 461.
40. *Ibid.*, 45.

glimpsed, do predominate in the theological symbolization that draws on family figures and relationships. We have already seen how the concept of the "fathers," in the sense of ancestors, is inseparable from the idea of the experience of God's salvation. The word "father" symbolizes, in the full sense of that term, the saving element in history; it recalls the past as the experience of God, in summons, promise, deliverance, and gift. As part of this kind of thinking the human representatives of God are often called "father." This is particularly so with the prophets and the wise men. Elisha calls Elijah "My father" (2 Kings 2:12), King Jehoash calls Elisha "My father" (2 Kings 13:14).[41] In the wisdom literature the instructor is conventionally a father and the hearer a son (Prov. 1:8; 4:1). In Judg. 18:19, the Danites invite Micah's Levite to come with them and be their "priest and father" and in Gen. 45:8 Joseph is a "father to Pharaoh" in his capacity as the counselor who brings God's will to Pharaoh. Thus, just as "the fathers" symbolizes the experience of God's grace, so those who are the channels of that grace are called father.

If "father" (mother) is a symbol of God's grace we might ask how this grace is understood by means of the symbol, and we might ask what the symbol means. A father had several major roles in the life of his children; he was obviously provider; in addition he was chiefly responsible for the religious instruction (Deut. 6:20–24; Ps. 78:3–7) and obedience of his family to the divine ordinances (Gen. 18:19). Fathers and sons were bound up together in their religious life, and the transgressions of the fathers had an effect on the sons (Jer. 16:10–12; Ezek. 18:2–20; Exod. 20:5). This is the negative expression of the same principle at work in the notion of the fathers as a conduit of blessing to their descendants; they could just as well transmit Yahweh's curse as his blessing. However, the association of the fathers with blessing and salvation so overshadows the opposite association that the symbolization is not affected: "Father" is still the symbol of salvation; and salvation comes as instruction to which one must be obedient. The element of authority is clearly present in the Israelite father's (mother's) relation to his children, but it is always exercised within the context of a prior gift and commitment

41. J. G. Williams, "The Prophetic Father," *JBL* 85 (1966) 344–8.

of life and nourishment, of parental love. Hence, it is no unreasonable authority, but rather a just claim, commensurate with the reality of the relationship. From the point of view of the father, it is based on justice; from the point of view of the child, the authority of the father is based on the child's own gratitude for present and remembered gifts. Paternal authority is a combination of firmness (Prov. 13:24; cf. 3:11–12) and compassion (Ps. 103:13), even as divine authority. For the pattern of gift and task, of demand within a context of succor, is precisely the pattern of Mosaic faith, in which the divine law was given on the basis of the divine gift of liberation from Egyptian slavery (Exod. 20:1). When Deuteronomy says that God bore the people from Egypt through the wilderness, "as a father carries his son" (Deut. 1:31), it evokes precisely the situation in a family: the parental succor which is the basis of the parental claim to authority. The family precedes the demand as the covenant precedes the law.[42]

At this point we might naturally introduce the passages in which God is not merely implied but rather explicitly declared to be a father, for every declaration of God as Father of the people occurs either in an indictment of Israel's ingratitude or as the basis of a plea for forgiveness in the face of an indictment.[43] Indeed, the theory we hope to prove is that the declaration of God as Father was a prophetic device, like the image of the cuckolded husband, for summing up the good that God had done and continued to do for his people, in order to provide a foil for their ingratitude or a basis for their plea for pardon. God their Father had saved them from bondage and given them the land; how ashamed they must be to turn against so generous a God! It is not a matter of a mere broken agreement; the same element of pathos as the cry of the betrayed husband evokes is present in the complaint of the dishonored father, as we might gather from the Bible's vivid portrayals of paternal love; the

42. F. Charles Fensham, "Father and Son as Terminology for Treaty and Covenant" in *Near Eastern Studies in Honor of W. F. Albright*, ed. H. Goedicke (Baltimore: Johns Hopkins, 1971) 121–135, argues that the "Father" symbol is an original part of the covenant idea.

43. The one exception (Jer. 31:9) is part of the promise of restoration after punishment. The occurrences in which God is father of an individual are in the Messianic oracle and its parallels (2 Sam. 7:14 etc.), and even there it is not free from the associations of indictment and punishment.

anguish of Jacob at the loss of Joseph and his passionate love for
Benjamin (Gen. 37:34–6; 42:36–38), David's concern for the child of
Bathsheba (2 Sam. 12:15–25), and his unforgettable lament for his
incorrigible Absalom: "O my son! Absalom my son, my son Absalom! If only I had died instead of you! O Absalom my son, my
son" (2 Sam. 18:33 and 19:4). This passionate dimension of fatherhood is also present in the prophetic declaration that God is a father
to Israel.[44]

The texts in question all come from the prophetic movement, and
most of them from the period just before and after the fall of Jerusalem in 586 B.C. Our first example, the so-called "Song of Moses"
(Deut. 32:1–43), is dated by von Rad in the period of the exile.[45]
The song may be divided into 7 sections: (i) Invocation (1–4) including a standard call from a "Wisdom" teacher to hear the teaching (vv. 1–2), and a declaration of the perfection of God's creation
and the truth of his justice (vv. 3–4); (ii) indictment of Israel (vv.
5–18) as a perverse people who show by this perversity that they are
not the children of this perfect creator: ". . . is this how you repay
the Lord, you brutish and stupid people? Is he not the father who
formed [qana] you? Did he not make you and establish you?" (v. 6).
This is followed by a recitation of the history of God's saving acts,
which opens with the invitation to "Remember the days of old,
think of the generations long ago; ask your father to recount it and
your elders to tell you the tale" (v. 7); then we are told that Yahweh
chose Israel for his own special care in the creation, "found"
(adopted) them in the wilderness, led and fed them; until they became spoiled children and rebellious, and roused his jealousy by
idolatry; they forsook "the rock who begot them" (male) and "the
God who gave [them] birth" (female) (v. 18). The indictment is
therefore essentially a recitation of God's saving acts bracketed by
the accusations that the people have forsaken the God who showed
himself to be their father and mother in creation and salvation. The
parental image is repeated in the recitation of the saving history,

---

44. Cf. D. A. Köberle, "Vatergott, Väterlichkeit und Vaterkomplex im christlichen
Glauben" in *Vorträge über das Vaterproblem in Psychotherapie, Religion und
Gesellschaft,* ed. W. Bitter (Stuttgart: Hippocrates, 1954) 17–18.
45. *Deuteronomy, A Commentary;* cf. G. E. Wright, "The Lawsuit of God: a
Form-critical Study of Deut. 32" in *Israel's Prophetic Heritage, Essays in Honor
of James Muilenburg,* ed. B. W. Anderson and W. Harrelson (New York: Harper
and Row, 1962) 26–67.

when in v. 11 Yahweh is presented like an eagle who watches over
its nest in his guarding of his people in the wilderness.

The other sections of the Song— (iii) punishment, God's angry response, vv. 19–25; (iv) transition to indictment of foreign nations,
vv. 26–30; (v) indictment of foreign nations, vv. 31–35; (vi) Israel's
restoration, vv. 36–38; (vii) God's power to punish his enemies and
to avenge his people, vv. 39–43—need only to be mentioned. The
Song shows the influence of the Wisdom tradition (vv. 1–2, 29), and
since the Wisdom tradition is known for its special interest in creation, this influence probably explains why in this text God is father
primarily because he is Israel's creator, and only subsequently because he is their redeemer. The word used in v. 6 for "to create,
form" (*qānā*) is relatively rare, and its best known occurrence in the
Old Testament is in the relatively late Wisdom passage, Prov. 8:22 ff.
("The Lord created [*qānā*] me the beginning of his works," v. 22).
The statement that Yahweh "found" them in the wilderness (cf.
Hos. 9:10), although it comes from a tradition other than those of
the "fathers" or the exodus, is present here to exclude the interpretation that because the relationship goes back to creation there is a
necessary (mythological) link between Yahweh and his people. The
link is contingent, and this "finding" is the sign that Yahweh
adopted them. Clearly, therefore, the fatherhood of God is a foil to
the sin of Israel; by worshipping other Gods they show ingratitude
and treachery, and above all stupidity in not acknowledging Yahweh
as creator and redeemer (vv. 6, 16–18).

The declarations of God as Father in Jeremiah 3 both occur in
indictments of Israel's sin, whose primary imagery is of the unfaithful wife; but there are other images drawn from the family. In v. 4,
Israel is the wayward daughter: "Not so long since, you called me
'Father, dear friend of my youth,' thinking, 'Will he be angry for
ever?' " The imagery drawn from family relationships, which controls the passage, is easily manipulated from wife to son. In vv. 19–20,

> I said, How gladly would I treat you as a son, giving you a pleasant
> land, a patrimony fairer than that of any nation! I said, You shall call
> me Father and never cease to follow me. But like a woman who is
> unfaithful to her lover, so you, Israel, were unfaithful to me,

the mixing of the two types of family imagery is clear, as is the
function of the idea of God's fatherhood in an indictment, and also
its link to the notion of the land "sworn on oath" to the fathers.

God as Father implies that the land is Israel's patrimony (cf. Deut. 12:9).

The father symbol is not only a foil for the indictment, but also a basis for the plea for pardon. In Trito-Isaiah we approach an invocation of God as Father, but do not quite reach it. In Isa. 64:8–9, "But now, Lord, thou art our father; we are the clay, thou art the potter, and all of us are thy handiwork. Do not be angry beyond measure, O Lord . . ." and Isa. 63:16, "Stand not aloof; for thou art our father, though Abraham does not know us nor Israel acknowledge us. Thou, Lord, art our father; thy name is our Ransomer from of old." The fatherhood of God is the basis on which Israel makes his plea for pardon and relief. The context of the father declaration here is still the sins of the people, however now the declaration is used to ask for forgiveness rather than to sharpen the indictment. In the Deuteronomy and Jeremiah passages God uses the declaration to make clear the reasonableness of his wrath; here the people use it to show the reasonableness of their request for pardon. They appeal to God as Father in the light of their experience of him as creator who determines their lives in every aspect, and as the redeemer, whose care for them in history surpasses that of their own fathers Abraham and Israel. This latter note suggests that Yahweh is more of a father than any earthly father can be, and the need not only to understand God by means of the father symbol but vice versa also. It also recalls how the "fathers" are in large measure constituted such by their function as mediators of God's grace.

The declaration of God as Father in Trito-Isaiah has already brought us to the verge of the New Testament in which he is invoked as such. There are other texts which bring the father symbol to the borders of the New Testament, those which tell of the hope for the final restoration, and those concerning the Messiah. Jer. 31:9 is part of the eschatological promise; the reason why, ". . . 'I will comfort them and be their escort, I will lead them to flowing streams; they shall not stumble, their path will be smooth'" is because "I have become a father to Israel, and Ephraim is my eldest son." God's fatherhood is the basis for the promise of final restoration (Jer. 31:20; Hos. 2:1).

The Messianic texts are those concerning the anointed Davidic

king. They all go back to the Nathan oracle in 2 Sam. 7:8–16, especially 14 (cf. 1 Chron. 17:13; 22:10; 28:6; Ps. 2:7; 89:26), which records
God's promise to maintain David's descendants on his throne. In New
Testament times the restoration of the Davidic monarchy, of the
anointed one or Messiah, was a mark of the final fulfillment of God's
purpose in history, which the Christians believed was achieved in
Jesus. Thus the Messianic oracle in 2 Samuel 7 points to the New
Testament and belongs among the later eschatological texts. At the
time of its formulation, however, it proclaims a father-son relationship between God and the king. "I will be his father, and he shall
be my son. When he does wrong I will punish him as any father
might and not spare the rod" (2 Sam. 7:14). This is based not on
any mythological idea of divine paternity for the king, but on the
idea of the king's adoption by God. Ps. 2:7, "You are my son . . .
This day I become your father," is an adoption formula that was
part of the coronation ceremony of the Davidic kings and was probably borrowed from Babylon.[46] It includes the idea of the king as
the people's representative and of the divine blessing being given to
individuals by virtue of their membership in the kingdom. In this
sense the Messianic texts are merely one more example of the father
symbolization we have already considered. The fact that the oracle
includes the threat of punishment confirms the impression. "When
he does wrong I will punish him as any father might and not spare
the rod" (2 Sam. 7:14)[47] places the oracle in the same frame of reference as the other "father" texts, namely, the people will be punished
(or forgiven) because God is their father.

The direct symbolization of God as Father in the prophetic texts
is more aptly described as a symbolization of God as parent, despite
the use of the word "father." Indeed, the predominant meaning of
the symbol as a ground for God's indictment of Israel suggests the
modern "Jewish mother" syndrome. "After all that I have done for
you, all my worrying, all my chicken soup, how could you be so
ungrateful?" is a fair translation of God's message to his children.

46. S. Mowinckel, *He That Cometh*, trans. G. W. Anderson (New York: Abingdon,
1954) 37; *The Psalms in Israel's Worship*, trans. D. R. Ap-Thomas, vol. 1 (New
York: Abingdon, 1962) 62 ff.
47. The reference to discipline recalls Prov. 13:24: "A father who spares the rod
hates his son, but one who loves him keeps him in order."

At the stage of indirect symbolization the message was: Break the original kinship ties, declare your independence, and then enter into a mature relationship with God based on an agreed covenant. The stage of direct symbolization occurs when that covenant has been violated and God's prophets have to remind the people of their obligation. There is passion in God's parental pleading—he is not merely interested in restoring a business agreement—and a hint of manipulation, but that belongs to the psychology rather than the theology of the symbol. Prophetic rhetoric appeals to the emotions, prophetic theology presumes that the hidden meaning of Israel's history is that God has chosen (adopted) this people and will remain true to them to the end, like a good parent; that God expects them to behave with mature responsibility in the relationship; and that the people can appeal to these theological facts as the grounds for repentance and the hope of forgiveness.

Jesus' religious heritage began with the shift in the locus of divine revelation from sacred place to special person, to the head of the family, characterized by us as the shift from the father of the gods to the God of the fathers. Concomitant with this was a change in the way the relationship with God was conceived, from a "natural" one in which the god is the progenitor of his people, to a free, intentional relationship based on call, election and covenant. This is emphasized in the religion of Moses, which developed and changed elements in the original patriarchal religion. The Mosaic stage identified the experience of deliverance from slavery in Egypt, the Exodus, as the moment when God elected Israel, and it describes this moment as an adoption. The Deuteronomists, part of the prophetic movement, beginning in the eighth century, emphasized the element of promise in the fathers' experience of God, specifically the promise of the land. "Fathers" symbolized for them the grace of God which gave them the land in which they lived.

All of the symbolization up to this point is "indirect," that is, symbolization by association. God is identified by association with the fathers. When, however, the prophets take up the idea of God and his relationship to the fathers, they identify God as Father by means of metaphor and simile. Such identification was implied in the Mosaic stage, in the references to Israel as God's son (Exod. 4:22b–23), but not stated explicitly. Among the prophets, God is called father directly, in order to emphasize his care for his people, as a foil to their sin—sin as an expression of ingratitude. Throughout the prophetic stage, whether the symbolization is direct or indirect, explicit or implied, there is a tendency to move back and forth between "father" and "mother" imagery. The symbol, therefore, is best described as that of "parent," with a preponderance of the "father" element.

Thus we have a symbol of free relationship and divine kindness in "father" as used of God in the Old Testament. These contents remained and were emphasized when Jesus used the symbol to present his experience of God.

CHAPTER 3

God the Father

in the

Teaching of Jesus

Anyone who would write about the teaching of Jesus must first deal with the problem of ascertaining what that teaching was. Modern scholarship has demonstrated that the records we have in the Gospels are an amalgam of the words of Jesus with sayings that were first formulated in the early communities of his followers, and then attributed to him. This phenomenon is not surprising when one considers that Jesus was not a figure of the past for his followers, but a living presence. He had risen from the dead and was spiritually present in his communities; his apostles and prophets spoke words inspired by his spirit, and since no strict distinction was made between the remembered words of the historical Jesus and the inspired words of the risen Christ, the tradition contains both kinds of material indiscriminately. It is not necessary for our purposes to consider the methodological niceties involved in the task of sifting the teaching of the historical Jesus from the tradition, but some introduction to the endeavor would be helpful.

The synoptic Gospels of Matthew, Mark, and Luke are our primary written sources, John being so heavily freighted with community interpretation as to make the task of sifting virtually impossible. The synoptics are made up of four types of written material: Mark, which is the earliest source, copied extensively by both Matthew and Luke; material common to Matthew and Luke but not found in Mark, which they may have gotten from one another (Luke copying Matthew or vice versa) or from a hypothetical third source (called in scholarly jargon Q); material peculiar to Matthew; and material peculiar to Luke. Behind these four written sources lies the putative oral tradition in which the sayings of the historical

Jesus were carried by word of mouth and mixed with sayings newly formed in the tradition. Finally, each of the evangelists arranged the material he received, both written and oral, so as to express his own view of the theological meaning of Jesus.

Imbedded in this three-layered evidence are sayings of the historical Jesus, and in order to identify them three criteria of judgment may be applied to the earliest form of the saying that can be recovered from a reconstruction of the history of the tradition. These criteria are most conveniently explained in Norman Perrin's important book *Rediscovering the Teaching of Jesus*.[1] The first and fundamental criterion is the criterion of dissimilarity, and it holds that sayings and parables which can be shown to be dissimilar to characteristic emphases in both the Judaism of Jesus' time and in early Christianity are probably from the mouth of Jesus. This is a minimalist criterion, since it excludes those sayings in which Jesus might have repeated elements from his religious heritage, and those which the church might have taken over from Jesus; and both kinds of sayings were surely on his lips. Nevertheless, in its scientific austerity the criterion of dissimilarity is the surest place to start in seeking to recover the teaching of Jesus. The second criterion, of multiple attestation, holds that themes and concerns which occur in different forms in the tradition may be accepted. For example, the concern for "tax collectors and sinners" is expressed in sayings, parables and controversy stories and is therefore authentic. The third criterion, of coherence, holds that material which is consistent with that which is guaranteed by the other two criteria might also be admitted. These are criteria of judgment and not substitutes for it; one still has to use educated discrimination, as in any historiography. We are convinced that the sayings upon which our reconstruction of Jesus' teaching on God the Father is based qualify as authentic by these criteria.

In order to understand not only the grounds for this judgment but also the full force of Jesus' message, it is necessary to know something about the teaching of contemporary Judaism on the fatherhood of God.[2] In the Palestinian sources collected under the title *Apocrypha and Pseudepigrapha*, dating from the first century

1. (New York: Harper and Row, 1967) 15–53.
2. For the following we are indebted to J. Jeremias, *Abba*, 19 ff.

B.C., the term "father" is used relatively infrequently of God—in all, only six times.[3] In the Hellenistic sources from the same collection it occurs seven times.[4] In the rabbinic sources, which are notoriously hard to date, it occurs more frequently, especially after Johanan ben Zakkai (ca. A.D. 50–80) began to favor the phrases "our heavenly father" and "Israel's heavenly father." The appellation was used to teach that one is obliged to obey God as a child does a father;[5] that God is a helper in time of need,[6] and a forgiver of sins.[7] On a few occasions the father appellation expresses an intimacy between God and the individual, which is new in comparison with the Old Testament, as in Sirach 51:10, "You are my father." In Hellenistic Judaism a sentimentalizing tendency is present,[8] which Palestinian Judaism does not evidence. Finally, although the term "our father and our king" is used as an invocation in prayer, the simple invocation "Father" does not occur in the extant prayer sources.[9] Therefore, although early Judaism differs from the Old Testament by invoking God as Father, this invocation does not indicate a personal intimacy with God, of the kind which is the hallmark of Jesus' use of "father" in his prayers.

---

3. R. H. Charles, *The Apocrypha and Pseudepigrapha of the Old Testament*, 2 vols. (Oxford: Clarendon, 1913) : Tob. 13:4; Sirach 51:10 (Hebrew) ; Jub. 1:24, 28; 19:29; Dead Sea Scrolls, 1 QH 9:35.

4. 3 Macc. 5:7; 6:3; 7:6; Wisd. of Sol. 2:16; 11:10; 14:3.

5. E.g. *Sifra Leviticus* to 20:26, "One does not say, 'I have no desire to wear cloth of mixed fibre, to eat pork, or to have sexual relations with a forbidden woman,' rather (one says) 'I do indeed desire to do such things, but how can I, since my heavenly father has forbidden me?' "

6. E.g. 1 QH 9:35 ff.:
My father does not know me,
And in comparison with you my mother has left me.
But you are the father of all your faithful
And rejoice over them as a loving mother over
    her baby,
And like a foster-father you cherish in your
    bosom all your creatures.

7. Tg Yer. I Lev. 22:28, "As your father in heaven is merciful so be merciful on earth."

8. E.g. *Joseph and Asenath* 12:14 ff., "You alone, Lord, are a father sweet, good and gentle. For what other father is sweet and good like you, Lord?"

9. The apparent attestation in Sirach 23:1 and 4, "Lord, father and master of my life" (1) and "Lord, father and God of my life" (4) is a mistranslation of the Hebrew, and should read, "God of my father and master of my life" and "God of my father and God of my life."

THE CARPENTER'S SON:
JESUS AND THE PATRIARCHY

Jesus' identity as "the son" is constituted by his relationship to God as the father; this is the unanimous witness of the traditions. In representing his most intimate understanding of God by the symbol "father" Jesus drew not only on religious tradition, but also on his own family experience. What was life like in such a family, and what was Jesus' attitude towards it?

The patriarchal order which we know from the Old Testament was still in force in Palestine.[10] The commandment to honor one's parents (Exod. 20:12) was one of the most important, and the position of the man with reference to his wife was regulated by texts such as Gen. 3:16 ("he shall be your master"). A man therefore had authority within his household over his wife, children, and other members. The social status of women in general was low; and the religious tradition was particularly cruel, suggesting that women were ontologically inferior to men. In the time of Jesus the pious man thanked God in his morning prayers that he had not been created "a Gentile, a woman, or as one unschooled in Judaism."[11] Under the law women were classed with minor children, slaves, Gentiles, and idiots, obliged to observe all prohibitions but not all injunctions; indeed, there are only three injunctions which women had to obey without exception: the proper purifications after menstruation, the conscientious removal of yeast from the house at Passover, and the lighting of the Sabbath candles.[12] Women were not taught the Torah ("The words of the Torah should rather be burnt than taught to women"—R. Eliezer, A.D. 90, Jer. Sota 19a, 8), they could not enter the inner courts of the temple, and they did not count in the synagogue towards the quorum of ten souls required for worship. Women could not be witnesses in a court of law. (How remarkable then that the Resurrection traditions make women the primary witnesses!) A famous rabbinic saying, "Do not speak much

---

10. Werner Foerster, *Neutestamentliche Zeitgeschichte* (Hamburg: Furche, 1968) 93–102.

11. K. H. Rengstorf, "Mann und Frau im Urchristentum," *Arbeitsgemeinschaft für Forschung des Landes Nordrhein-Westfalen*, Geisteswissenschaften 12 (Cologne und Oplanden: Westdeutscher, 1954, 7–52) 11–12.

12. *Ibid.*, 12.

with a woman," was interpreted as applying specifically to conver-
sation with one's wife (Pir. Aboth 1:5; cf. John 4:27). Under these
circumstances it was no small matter that Jesus had women in his
company of followers, and seems to have spoken with them openly
and often.[13]

The baleful effects of patriarchalism were also evident in marriage law. Under the rubric of Gen. 3:16, "You shall be eager for
your husband, and he shall be your master," the man was the active
agent: he married or divorced the woman, she was married or divorced. Her father had the authority to give her in marriage, a
transaction by which she passed from the power of her father into
the power of her husband. The bargain was based on a threefold
contract regulating the dowry that remained in possession of the
woman, the dowry that passed to the man, and the agreement
(*kethuba*) on how much was to be paid to the woman if her husband
divorced her or died. The *kethuba* was the only real defence a
woman had against capricious divorce, although some rabbis did
make the form of the required letter of divorce so complex that its
preparation caused a delay during which the husband might re-
consider. Nevertheless, divorce governed by Deut. 24:1[14] was easy,
and at the man's discretion. The rabbinic schools argued about the
meaning of "something shameful," the cause allowed in Deut. 24:1,
Shammai holding that only adultery qualified, while Hillel allowed
a wide range of possibly shameful things. The age of marriage was
usually 18–24 years for the boy and 13–14 years for the girl; it was
a duty for a man to marry rather than remain single. In the light
of this, it is noteworthy that Jesus forbade divorce, and that at the
probable age of thirty he was apparently unmarried.

The father was, therefore, the supreme authority in the family,
and the subordination of wife and children was definite and evident (cf. Luke 2:51). One custom which made this vividly apparent
was that in return for his feeding, clothing, and supporting her, a
woman was obliged not only to render the usual domestic and sexual
service but specifically to wash her husband's feet, a task to which a

13. Jewett, *Man as Male and Female.*
14. "When a man has married a wife, but she does not win his favor because
he finds something shameful in her, and he writes her a note of divorce, gives
it to her and dismisses her . . ."

slave could not legally be compelled.[15] With reference to his daughters, the father's chief concern was to transfer them to their eventual husbands without blemish; to his sons his obligations were more extensive. He was responsible for teaching his sons the law and customs of religion, and, in the level of society to which Jesus belonged, he introduced his sons to the secrets of his trade. If Joseph was indeed a carpenter, he would have initiated Jesus into the skills of carpentry. At all times the son owed his father obedience, and in their old age he owed both parents support and care.

From the point of view of a modern understanding of human rights, the position of women in this patriarchate is shameful. It does nothing to mitigate this judgment that Rengstorf can find an early example of the anti-feminine morning prayer in Greek sources,[16] although his claim that such chauvinism entered Judaism only as a result of Greek influence is worth serious consideration, in view of John Otwell's interpretation of the Old Testament evidence as giving women relatively favorable status.

Since the New Testament is as much a product of the Greco-Roman world as it is of Judaism, we must also consider the family structure in this larger world.[17] The family was much less stable at the turn of the age than it had ever been before. Indeed, that situation has been compared with our own; the rate of divorce was high, the reputation of fidelity low. Children were a nuisance, and infant exposure, a rudimentary alternative to abortion, was widely practised. The evidence we have shows that while children in general were undesirable, female children were more so than male. At one time in the second century B.C. in Miletus, seventy-nine families had a total of one hundred and eighteen sons and twenty-eight daughters—1.8 children per family, with a figure for female children which shows that they were exposed at a rate four times that of the males. A letter from an Egyptian laborer to his wife, from the first century B.C., states bluntly that if their expected child is a son he is to be kept, if a daughter, exposed.[18] Unwanted children were left

---

15. Foerster, *Zeitgeschichte*, 96.

16. Thales of Miletus is reported to have thanked the goddess of fortune that "he was born a human and not an animal, a man and not a woman, a Greek and not a barbarian," *"Mann und Frau,"* 14, n. 18.

17. Foerster, *Zeitgeschichte*, 201–209.

18. *Ibid.*, 208.

exposed in the wilderness or on the garbage heaps of the cities, to starve or be eaten by wild animals—or to be collected by pimps, psychopaths, or slave-traders. In favor of the Jewish patriarchy it must be said that the murder of children was strictly prohibited.

In traditional Rome, before the corruptions of the empire, a father had the right of life and death over his children. He could expose them, sell them, or kill them. The wife had the legal status of a daughter and so was subject to the same absolute authority, although her husband could only punish her with the consent of the council of the extended family. Marriage took place by a solemn ceremony before witnesses; the wife and her goods passed into the possession of the husband; divorce was impossible. Men married at 18–20 years of age, women at 13–15 years. A wife's status was reasonably high within the family, she took part in the council, received visitors, and appeared in public.

During the empire another form of marriage became popular, in which a woman did not pass under the authority of her husband, but remained under that of her father. Her husband, therefore, could not gain access to her fortune, and divorce was a relatively easy matter. Under this arrangement Caesar had four wives in relatively rapid succession, and Sulla and Pompey five each. Such a marriage without "authority" probably explains why adultery was taken lightly and indulged in heavily.

The Greek contribution to the marital life of the empire was the "romantic and aesthetic nimbus"[19] with which the Greeks adorned extra-marital sexual relations. Since in Athens a wife was confined to the women's quarter of the house and played no part in male society, Athenian males cultivated the society of the *Heterai* and beautiful boys for sexual pleasure. *Heterai* were, like the Geishas of pre-modern Japan, the women with most education and social grace; they provided what the Greeks in Foerster's inimitable phrase loved most, "erotically tinged intellectual play." The boys, of course, attest the well-known preference of the intellectual Greek for pederasty. They regarded homosexual love as a mark of civilization—like athletics and philosophy—for which the barbarians had no appreciation, precisely because they were barbarians.[20] As

19. *Ibid.*, 204.
20. Cf. Plato, *Symposium*, 7 and 9.

Plato wrote, those possessed by eros in general, love both women and men, but those inspired by the divine eros "devote themselves to the male, because they love by nature that which is stronger and thinks most clearly" (Symp. 9). Dancing girls and pleasure boys found their way into the lives of the upper-class Romans, albeit without the refined rationalizations of the Greeks.

Philosophy did, however, make its impact on the relations between the sexes. Most widespread was the idea that a man should love his wife rationally—a union of mind and soul as it were—and save his passion for slave-girls. Also popular was the idea that marriage, not being found among the animals, was contrary to nature. In sum, philosophy contributed to the misery rather than the joy of marriage. The censor Metellus Numidicus advised his fellow-citizens, since nature has decreed that men can live neither with nor without women, they should think of the welfare of society at large and shoulder the burden of marriage manfully. This is surely tongue-in-cheek advice; there were many who found the promised bliss as the following gravestone testifies: "She never hurt me; except by dying."[21]

The status of women in the Greco-Roman world appears, by modern standards, to have been better than in Judaism. If Plato justified pederasty by denigrating the feminine soul, he and his successors also saw that men and women possessed reason in common. By the time of the New Testament women were admitted to the study of philosophy, and some thinkers advocated equal education for girls and boys. The frequency of divorce, the sexual adventures of married women, the marriage in which a woman retained her possessions, all testify to an independence for women which has no parallel in Judaism. Clearly the Greco-Roman patriarchy was in trouble, and no alternative was in sight. The New Testament set itself against this aspect of the Gentile world with a fervor: divorce, sexual license, pederasty, adultery, and any form of lewdness were roundly condemned (e.g. 1 Cor. 6:9–10; Gal. 6:19–21). In much of this opposition the Christians made common cause with the Greek-speaking Jews and philosophers like the Cynics and Stoics. Christianity therefore inherited its view of the father's power and privilege from both its parents, from Athens and Jerusalem, and although

21. Foerster, *Zeitgeschichte*, 206.

the New Testament contains the seeds of its destruction, Christianity perpetuated the patriarchy.

The New Testament suggests, however, that there was a serious ambivalence in the early Christian attitude towards the father's authority. It is most evident in the sayings about the status of women, which express contempt (1 Cor. 14:34) and unparalleled affirmation (Gal. 3:28) at the same time. This situation represents the confrontation between the impulse for reformation of the patriarchy on the one hand, which we hope to show emanated from Jesus, and the resistance of entrenched privilege on the other. Jesus broke the forms of the patriarchal family in the name of God the Father, and recognized the natural right of women to equal humanity with men. The records of his life are clear in their witness: he had women in his entourage (Mark 15:40–41), he spoke with women in public (John 4:27), spent time teaching them (Luke 10:39); and in a breathtaking scene, whose full significance has yet to be understood, he let a whore wash his feet, let her perform a service for him which was the characteristic sign of a wife's duty to her husband (Luke 7:36–38). He paid special attention to mothers and children, over the characteristic objections of his disciples (Mark 10:13–16),[22] and he refused to condemn an adulteress, knowing how unfair the law on adultery was to women, upon whom alone it laid the obligation of absolute marital fidelity; he refused to be a part of the "double standard" (John 7:53–8:11). He forbade divorce, and based the marriage relationship on the "one flesh" idea of Gen. 2:24, an idea which allows neither the subordination of one partner to the other nor the treating of the woman as a chattel whose adultery infringes the man's property rights. Finally, it was to women that he entrusted the initial witness to his Resurrection, because only women-followers stood by his cross (Mark 15:47–16:8).

The evidence that Jesus recognized the natural rights to which their humanity entitled women is clear, and especially moving when considered against the background of the regnant patriarchy. Against all custom (and in violation of specific injunctions) he made women his friends, taught them Torah (Luke 10:38–42), spent time with them in public and in private, and entrusted to them his single

---

22. Cf. Milan Machovec, *A Marxist Looks at Jesus* (Philadelphia: Fortress, 1976) 99, "That a child should be put forward as an example is something quite new in the history of religions and equally new in the history of cultures."

most important task, the witness to his Resurrection. The price he paid for this fearless love was his own life; and before that final reckoning he lost his family and his respectability (Mark 3:31–35). He was crucified because he contravened the religious law in the name of God who gave the law. His contraventions were all in favor of those whom the law oppressed—the "people of the land" who were ritually unclean because of their daily work, the whores and tax officials who collaborated with the occupation forces, the women and children who were at the disposal of their men. The heart of his message, in word and deed, was that God is a father who frees us from oppression by including us in his family; that when God's will is done on earth all will be included and none excluded; that his fatherly care means equal dignity and worth for all. This message was a threat not only to the interests of a religion that used the law to establish an elite, but also to a society which used religion to oppress the weak. The impulse that went out from Jesus caused him to be crucified; it is not surprising that his followers tempered it to their times.

The harshest reaffirmations of patriarchal power in the New Testament occur in the later layers of the tradition. When these strata were formed the church was settling down to the long haul of history, realizing that they had been mistaken in thinking that Jesus had promised an imminent end to the world. The powers of the new age which had attended his teaching, and flashed forth in his Resurrection, had to be contained within the forms of the old. The new age and the old led a parallel existence in this strange time between the times; therefore social attitudes were bound to be ambivalent, formed as they were by influences from different worlds. On the one hand there is the brutal prohibition on women speaking in the congregation (1 Cor. 14:34–35);[23] the fatuous suggestion that women will be saved by bearing children (1 Tim. 2:15), and the fantastic connection of all this with the Adam and Eve story (1 Tim. 2:13–14; cf. 1 Cor. 11:2–3). There are also the direct injunctions to women to be subject to their husbands (1 Pet. 3:1; Col. 3:18; Eph. 5:23; Titus 2:5; 1 Cor. 14:34), which occur in lists of household virtues reminiscent of the moralizing plaques in Vic-

---

23. This is an intrusion into 1 Corinthians from the later Deutero-Pauline tradition. It is not from the apostle. Cf. 1 Tim. 2:11–12. Thus Robin Scroggs, "Paul and the Eschatological Woman." *JAAR* 40 (1972) 282–303.

torian parlors, on which Kipling's poem "If" was a favorite goad to guilt and greater things. On the other hand, however, we find Gal. 3:28, "There is no such thing as Jew and Greek, slave and freeman, male and female, for you are all one person in Christ Jesus"; and some of the household tables show a new awareness of the limits of patriarchal power. For instance, in Eph. 5:25 ff. (cf. Col. 3:18) a husband must love his wife as Christ loved the church, cherishing her as he does his own body, (cf. v. 31, the "one flesh" idea) ". . . in loving his wife a man loves himself" (v. 28). Children must honor and obey their parents as the fourth commandment states (6:1–3) but fathers are also under obligation to treat their children properly, not to "goad your children to resentment, but [to] give them the instruction, and the correction, which belong to a Christian up-bringing" (6:4). Love between husband and wife was not an important ingredient in the old patriarchal marriage; marriage was more a social than an emotional arrangement; indeed, some circles in Greece argued that the rudimentary state of the feminine soul made it impossible for a man to love a woman. (Possibly a pederast's rationalization.) All the more remarkable then is this emphasis on loving and cherishing one's wife; clearly Christianity contained forces which set limits to the old patriarchal power.

An especially vivid example of the ambivalence in early Christian attitudes to women (and therefore to patriarchy) occurs in 1 Corinthians 11.[24] The problem is the seemingly trivial one of whether a woman should wear a covering on her head when speaking in the congregation. This covering was a "sign of authority" (v. 10). Paul, who had written that in Christ there is no difference between male and female (Gal. 3:28), faced the fact that in the Corinthian congregation, or any of the congregations (v. 16), a woman who spoke without this veil would be in serious breach of custom and possibly the cause of scandal. He does not cut the Gordian knot, as we might have expected had he written 1 Cor. 14:34–35, and simply forbid women to speak at all. He accepts the fact that women address the congregation, and this alone is a significant change in the customs of

24. Cf. Scroggs, *ibid.*; and "Paul and the Eschatological Woman: Revisited," *JAAR* 42 (1974) 532–37; Elaine Pagels, "Paul and Women: A Response to Recent Discussion," *ibid.*, 538–49; Jerome Murphy-O'Connor, "The Non-Pauline Character of 1 Corinthians 11:2–16?" *JBL* 95 (1976) 615–21, which is a response, maintaining the Pauline authorship of our passage, to W. O. Walker who denies it in "1 Corinthians and Paul's Views Regarding Women," *JBL* 94 (1975) 94–110.

the patriarchy. Rather than attempt to revoke this new liberty, which would have been against his convictions, Paul tries to mount an argument for the custom of the veil. He summons Adam and Eve (cf. 1 Tim. 2:13–14) to testify that man was created before woman, and indeed that woman came out of man! On this basis he constructs a hierarchy with God at the top, woman at the bottom, and Christ and man in descending order in between. The covered head is a sign that woman is under man in this hierarchy. However, as he concludes this ridiculous argument about woman having come from man, his good sense and Christian conscience reassert themselves and Paul throws up his hands with:

> And yet, in Christ's fellowship woman is as essential to man as man is to woman. If woman was made out of man, it is through woman that man now comes to be; and God is the source of all (1 Cor. 11:11–12).

It is as if, having set out on an impossible mission—to justify the "sign of authority" upon women—he wishes the whole argument would self-destruct. Indeed, this concluding declaration of the reciprocity between man and woman in procreation and in the church and the final appeal to the one God who is the source of all effectively nullifies his foregoing argument and shows that he could not accommodate the impulse emanating from Jesus to existing privilege. In 1 Cor. 11:2–12 Paul used an existing argument (cf. 1 Tim. 2:13–14) for the order of society, and discovered in the course of presenting it, that it made no sense in the light of Jesus' new spirit. He rejected it, therefore, and appealed precipitately to nature (vv. 13–15) and to custom (v. 16); but such appeals are not arguments; they merely plunge Paul more deeply in the mire of ambiguity and inconsistency. Paul had no reason for supporting the custom of a "sign of authority" beyond the desire to conserve the existing order, and he suffered the embarrassment which all conservatives have to bear when challenged by reason.

Jesus had no such desire; his eyes were on the horizon, looking for the dawning of a new age whose energies he commanded in anticipation. His words and deeds, charged with these energies, frequently were in conflict with the existing order; and in no place was this more evident than in their impact on the patriarchal family. We have already seen how he ignored patriarchy's norms for the humiliation of women; now we must consider how he liberated the children.

The earliest sources in the synoptic Gospels, Mark and the hypothetical sayings source Q, are clear in their testimony that Jesus and his followers broke with their families. Mark 3:31–35 tells how Jesus' mother and his brothers stood outside a house where he was teaching, kept at a distance by the crowd, and sent a message for him to join them. This called forth the well-known response from Jesus:

> "Who is my mother? Who are my brothers?" And looking round at those who were sitting in the circle about him he said, "Here are my mother and my brothers. Whoever does the will of God is my brother, my sister, my mother!" (vv. 33–34).

3:20–21 is usually regarded as an introduction to this scene in which Jesus rejects his family. The *New English Bible* translates 3:21 as follows: "When his family heard of this [i.e. his being hemmed into a house by the crowd] they set out to take charge of him; for people were saying that he was out of his mind." This translation is misleading, however; the Greek which is translated "his family" is literally "those about him," and the whole sentence is more plausibly rendered, "And when those who were with him heard this [i.e. that the crowd was so thick he had no chance to eat] they went out to restrain it [the crowd], for they said, it is out of control."[25] There-

---

25. G. Hartmann, "Mark 3:20 f." in *Biblische Zeitschrift* 11 (1939) 249–79, as discussed in Hans Hartmut Schroeder, *Eltern und Kinder in der Verkündigung Jesu, Eine hermeneutische und exegetische Untersuchung*, Theologische Forschung 53 (Hamburg-Bergstedt: Herbert Reich, 1972) 110, n.8. On the general theme of Jesus' "itinerant radicalism" see Gerd Theissen, *Sociology of Early Palestinian Christianity*, trans. John Bowden (Philadelphia: Fortress, 1978) 7–30. He regards the theme of homelessness and lack of family to be an indication of the situation of the wandering charismatics who formed the elite leadership of the Jesus movement. In this respect, however, they are carrying on the mode of life of Jesus himself; there is a "structural homologue between the attitudes of the wandering charismatics and the local communities on the one hand and that of the Son of Man on the other" (26). Theissen says further that his sociological method "suggests that we should assume a continuity between Jesus and the Jesus movement and in so doing opens up the possibility of transferring insights into the Jesus movement to Jesus himself" (4). So sociological factors do not render the historical Jesus otiose in the explanation of the history of the Jesus movement, as more radical form critics tend to suggest. In sociological terms of the kind Theissen uses, Jesus' position as a wandering preacher without family ties is "marginal" and the outcasts of society to whom he appeals are likewise "marginal." Radical criticism of established society usually comes from marginal people; and the accommodation to the patriarchy by the church after Jesus represents the shift from the marginal values of the wandering charismatics to the values of settled people with social responsibility.

fore, 3:20–21 does not explain why his family came looking for him; it merely sets the circumstantial scene, of Jesus in a crowd and so not privately accessible. His family came to take him home not because he was apparently insane and thus an embarrassment to them; rather they came to remind him of his obligations as the eldest son under the patriarchy, to care for his mother and minor siblings. Even if vv. 31–35 portray an ideal rather than a real scene, the saying establishing his new family and breaking from his old is probably an accurate reflection of Jesus' intention, and it would have been understood as a rejection of his family obligations in favor of the Kingdom of God. In Luke's special material this point is also made, when the child Jesus, who had caused his parents anxiety by remaining behind in the city while the pilgrim caravan returned North, has the following exchange with them:

> . . . his mother said to him, "My son, why have you treated us like this? Your father and I have been searching for you in great anxiety." "What made you search?" he said. "Did you not know that I was bound to be in my father's house?" (Luke 2:48) .

The call of God the Father takes precedence over the summons of any earthly father, and justifies the breaking of family ties and the apparent neglect of natural obligations. Jesus' call brings a new family into being whose father is God and whose ties are the free adherence of faith. Not blood relationship but the doing of God's will makes one a member of God's family. This is confirmed in Q when John the Baptist warns his hearers not to say, "We have Abraham as our father," but to bring forth the fruits of repentance (Matt. 3:9 = Luke 3:8). Repentance is the breaking of natural ties, and following Jesus is the free enrolling in the new family of God. This pattern of change is by now familiar to us; an initial relationship (to God and family) based on natural kinship is broken and then restored on the basis of free choice and obedience. This free obedience to the heavenly Father constitutes all who give it a new family in faith.

Those who become disciples make the same renunciation as Jesus. Mark 1:20 tells us bluntly that James and John left their father Zebedee in the boat with the hired hands and went off with Jesus. This may be an ideal portrayal; but the curt retort in Q (Matt. 8:22 = Luke 9:60b) to the young man who wants to bury his father

before following Jesus has the eschatological astringency of a genuine Jesus-word: "Leave the dead to bury their dead; you must go
and announce the Kingdom of God" (Luke 9:60b). Both Luke and
Matthew place the saying at a strategic point in their treatment of
the meaning of discipleship. Luke has it at the beginning of the
long journey to Jerusalem which is the image by which he portrays
discipleship, namely, as the following after Jesus. Matthew has it
before the storm on the lake which tested the disciples' resolution
and found it wanting. Only Luke has the injunction, "Go and announce the Kingdom of God," and in this surely perceives the
source of the urgency implicit in the command. The call of the Kingdom of God brooks no excuse, no delay, and leaves in shreds the
ties that bind. The duty of a son to bury his dead father promptly
was solemn, and indeed, given the fact that a dead person had by
law to be buried the day after death, an urgent matter; but the call
of the Kingdom takes precedence. The setting of the saying—a young
man asking to be allowed to delay following Jesus until he has
performed his last and most solemn filial duty—may be a product
of the tradition; it may be a frame constructed for the enigmatic
word, "Leave the dead to bury their dead, and come follow me
[announce the Kingdom]." Be that as it may, it is an accurate expli-
cation of the saying's intention. Jesus not only renounced his own
family obligations but called others to do so as well.

An apparently hard saying on this theme occurs in Q: "If anyone
comes to me and does not hate his father and mother, wife and
children, brothers and sisters, even his own life, he cannot be a disciple of mine" (Luke 14:26 = Matt. 10:37–38).[26] Matthew changed
"hate" into "love more" in an effort to soften the impact of the
demand. The Greek "hate" is a translation of the Aramaic original
sānā, which means "to neglect or treat slightingly." It would seem
then that Matthew's change fortuitously produced a rendering closer
to the putative Aramaic original than the older Greek version of
Luke. What Jesus said was that a disciple has to place his love for
parents, spouse, siblings, and offspring second to his loyalty to the
Kingdom of God.

Mark 13:12–13 presents another saying of Jesus on the strains the
Kingdom places on the family. This time the subject is persecution,

26. Schroeder, *Eltern*, 92 ff.

rather than voluntary renunciation for the sake of the mission. "Brother will betray brother to death, and the father his child; children will turn against their parents and send them to their death" (v. 12).[27] Many commentators describe this saying as a "commonplace of apocalyptic expectations"; such persecution and mutual hostility is allegedly a standard element in the "woes" which are to precede the end of the world. However, Schroeder[28] can find only one example of such strife within the family in the apocalyptic literature we have from that time (2 Enoch 100:2). This hardly makes it a common idea. Rather than a commonplace we have here a prophecy of Jesus that the experience of his followers will be similar to his own experience of violence for the sake of the Kingdom of God (cf. Matt. 10:38 = Luke 14:27; John 15:18–21; Matt. 24:9; Matt. 5:11–12 = Luke 6:22). The later Christian community, in turn, interpreted the prophecy within the framework of apocalyptic expectation as one of the signs of the approaching end. Consonant with his intention, his followers perceived Jesus to be playing a decisive role in the final events, and so properly understood his experience of rejection and persecution to be one of the events leading to the in-breaking of God's reign. Far from being a commonplace, therefore, the verses about persecution and rejection within the family are a generalization from the experience of Jesus and his followers, probably based on a prophecy made by Jesus himself.

Finally, in Mark 10:28–30 we have evidence that people actually did leave their families and find in the church a substitute family. Peter said, "We here . . . have left everything to become your followers." Jesus said, "There is no one who has given up home, brothers, sisters, mother, father or children, or land, for my sake and for the gospel, who will not receive in this age a hundred times as much . . . and persecutions besides; and in the age to come eternal life." It is rather puzzling that the saying should promise such a high reward in this life. Some speculate that this is evidence of a 'Norman Vincent Pealism' in the early church; some circles were so enthusiastic about the Resurrection that they forgot the cross, and expected the power which raised Jesus to work for them, too, trans-

---

27. The saying also occurs in Q in a secondary formulation, which makes the allusion to Mic. 7:6 into a quotation (Matt. 10:34–6 = Luke 12:51–53).
28. Schroeder, *Eltern*, 134, n.7.

forming their sacrifices into success. The experience of persecution, possibly the Neronian onslaught of A.D. 65, reminded the Markan Christians that their master's fate in this world had been a cross; and so the Gospel was written as a theology of the cross, and only fragments of the early 'Pealism' remain in the traditions which comprise it. The discussion of which the saying is part concerns the question introduced in 10:10 by the rich young man: "Good master, what must I do to win eternal life?" Eternal life or the Kingdom of God is the issue for Mark, and reward in this world is secondary. We may safely set aside the section on earthly rewards as residue of an earlier misunderstanding—which alas, is still with us—namely, the delusion that faith in Jesus means success in this world. The rich young man could not meet the cost of discipleship, the price of eternal life; he could not put following Jesus before the claims and comforts of this world. Peter and the others had done so and their reward would be eternal life.

This saying about abandoning parents stands in proximity to a quotation of the fourth commandment on the lips of Jesus (10:19). Either it is entirely fortuitous that the pericope has Jesus quote the command to honor one's parents as part of his call to leave them and follow him, or it is of the greatest moment for understanding the message. In rabbinic tradition the love of God, of the Torah, and of one's teacher took precedence over the love of parents.[29] Jesus could, therefore, be appealing to the young man as a teacher to his pupil to put love of parents second to love of him. However, the issue at stake is eternal life, and this suggests that Jesus' appeal is based on something more important than the teacher-pupil relationship.

In Mark 7:9-13, Jesus attacks the Pharisees for the 'corban' custom, by which a man could evade his duty to support his aged parents. One did not actually have to deliver the goods pledged to religious ends under the corban vow; they merely became available to one's own use, free of obligation to parents. It might seem a contradiction that Jesus, who claimed for himself and his followers the right to abandon their parents, should castigate the Pharisees for doing the same thing. However, the issue is not whether the parents should be supported or not, it is rather the grounds on

29. *Ibid.,* 102.

which the claim to be free of that obligation is made. In the case of corban, it is the unwritten law which renders the written law inoperative; but Jesus does not accept the unwritten law in this case. "Thus by your own tradition, handed down among you, you make God's word null and void," he says (7:13). This implies that if God's word is to be changed or set aside, only God can do so. Jesus' call takes precedence over the fourth commandment, therefore, not merely because he is teacher or because his word is tradition like the words of other teachers, but because his call is the call of the kingdom, his word the word of God.

Thus the words of Jesus were an axe laid to the roots of the family tree; nevertheless, by force of habit, the knotty trunk still stands. We have seen how the writers of the New Testament were among those who rushed to the early defence of the patriarchate; how even a radical like Paul could not contemplate its passing. They were victims of the overlap of ages, the "already but not yet" of our time between the times. Schroeder claims that these words of Jesus against family authority should not be taken as norms for present behavior because Jesus spoke them to individuals. This is an evasion; Jesus proclaimed that the breaking of the bonds of human kinship was a revelation of God's sovereignty. When God is king no one will be bound to another by fate; only love will keep us together. Since love is by definition freely given and received, the true family will be constituted in freedom. ("Those who do the will of God are my mother and brothers.") This freedom is a characteristic of the kingdom, and even though it only comes to expression in individual instances, it is a universal truth. Not that we know it to be such beyond doubt, but we hypothesize that when the kingdom comes freedom will be vindicated. For the time being we must live with the passing patriarchy, not in dismay at the passing of the old order, but in expectancy of the new.

Ever since the advent of modern industrial society the family has been in process of change. Begemann characterizes it as a movement from patriarchy to partnership.[30] The household tables of primitive Christianity do not meet the needs of the modern

---

30. Helmut Begemann, *Strukturwandel der Familie, Eine sozialtheologische Untersuchung über den Strukturwandel von der patriarchalischen zur partner-schaftlichen Familie* (Hamburg: Furche, 1960).

family because its structure is different from such an early household. Questions about women's participation in the leadership of
the church are not really illuminated by the contortions of Paul in
1 Corinthians 11. The stream of history has flowed on by the
bulwarks which cowardice constructs against the kingdom. The
casuistry of Pauline compromise, the certainty of the pseudo-
apostolic Pastorals, are left behind like stony outcrops in the waters
of life; but the words of Jesus have not yet been reached. They are
the sea to which all rivers run, the ocean to which all things return.
We therefore welcome the fact that the family has been changing
from a patriarchy to a partnership under the impact of industrializa-
tion. Time has made the temporizing of Jesus' later interpreters
uncouth, and has vindicated his radicalism. If he did indeed speak
for the reign of God, as we believe, then we must judge the passage
from patriarchy to partnership to be the action of God in our history, for it conforms to the words of Jesus about the breaking and
reconstituting of family ties. It also corroborates Freud's Oedipal
insight, that family ties have to be broken for the child if he or she
is to be able to enter into the mature relationship which can only
be constituted after the break.

Such a judgment does not entail a simple doctrine of human
progress, as if all change were for the better. We are not arguing
that simply because partnership is later in history than patriarchy
it must be better. Our opinion is based rather on a matter-of-fact
consideration of the pertinent sayings of Jesus, and candid acceptance of the facts of contemporary history. The juxtaposition of
the two suggests that Jesus seems to have been right—so far, the
breaking of family ties which he called for does seem to be necessary for full maturity, and for genuine relationships. The process
of our history, the impact of industrialism and modernism seems to
be confirming rather than contradicting this aspect of Jesus'
teaching.

GOD'S SON: JESUS AND THE DIVINE FATHER

Jesus called people away from the bondage of kinship, the ties of
fate, to relationships based on freedom and joined in love. He did
so in the name of the "Kingdom of God," an awareness of the divine

purpose that is as mysterious as it is powerful. Nothing less than his whole life, culminating in the cross and vindicated by the Resurrection, could adequately express the meaning of the phrase "Kingdom of God," and then only provisionally. Nevertheless, there is one element in the teaching that takes us nearer than any other to the truth: Jesus called God "Father"; and because of that his followers called him "Son." Since there is this close connection between the kingdom and the fatherhood of God, we concentrate our inquiry on the Lord's Prayer; a prayer for the kingdom which invokes God as "Father."

The Lord's Prayer is only the best known instance of a strong tradition that "Father" was Jesus' special appellation for God. The term occurs 170 times on the lips of Jesus in the Gospels: Mark 4, Luke 15, Matthew 42, John 109.[31] The term occurs more frequently in the later traditions (Matthew and John). In Matthew the increase occurs in the pre-Matthean stage of the tradition, and is probably due to four factors: the general adoption of the appellation in the Judaism with which Matthew was associated, after its favoring by the influential Johanan ben Zakkai (ca. A.D. 50–80); the development of the catechetical tradition, in which most of Matthew's special occurrences are found (e.g. 6:1–18; 10:17–39; 18:10–35); its use in liturgy (as the Pauline instances show: 1 Cor. 8:6; Rom. 6:4; Col. 1:12; Eph. 2:18; 3:14); and its use by the early Christian prophets (Rev. 2:28; 3:5, 21). The Johannine tradition adopted it wholeheartedly as the Christian appellation for God. Therefore, the meaning of "Father" on the lips of Jesus is to be sought not in Matthew and John, but in the earlier sources, Mark, Q, and the special Lukan material.

The astonishing fact that in all five layers of the gospel tradition (Mark, Q, Matthew, Luke, and John) Jesus, with one exception, always invokes God as "Father" in his recorded prayers, directs our attention to the prayers. (The exception is the cry from the cross, "My God, my God, why hast thou forsaken me?" in Mark 15:34 = Matt. 27:46, which is a quotation of Ps. 22:1). The term Jesus used

---

31. Jeremias, *Abba* 33. In what follows we are indebted to this epoch-making article. See also, J. Jeremias, *New Testament Theology, The Proclamation of Jesus* (New York: Scribners, 1971) 61–67, 193–203.

is the Aramaic "Abba" (stress on the second syllable) as its quotation in Mark 14:36 (the Gethsemane prayer) and its use by Paul (Rom. 8:15; Gal. 4:6) show. The only reason why Mark and Paul, who were writing for Gentiles who knew no Aramaic, would quote this unintelligible word, is the undeniable tradition that it was indeed Jesus' special name for God.

"Abba" originated as a babble-word (German: *Lallform*) used by small children of their fathers. It is not inflected and takes none of the suffixes by which Aramaic indicates the personal and possessive pronouns. Thus "abba" can mean "father," "my father," "the father" etc., a fact which explains many of the variations in the New Testament form of the appellations. Although it originated with young children, it was used by adults of their fathers, and also as an address of courtesy to older men. It is, in brief, a word from the everyday speech of the family; and while our evidence shows that the Jews of Jesus' world never addressed God as "Abba," Jesus always did! Therefore, "Abba" is an actual word of the historical Jesus. It reveals the heart of his relationship to God, and therefore, the essence of the kingdom. "Abba" holds the key to Jesus' authority and identity.

We hear Jesus pray "Abba" for the first time in Gethsemane (Mark 14:36), where in trust he surrenders himself to God's will. The prayer in the garden is an ideal construction; it is unlikely that anyone would have heard Jesus pray; the attendant disciples were asleep, we are told! Nevertheless, it is not unlikely that Gethsemane was the actual scene of his agony and arrest, and that he prayed during the struggle. The tradition which supplied the words of the prayer is firmly based on the well-known fact that Jesus used "Abba" to invoke God, and that this meant total trust in him. The Gethsemane pericope does not give the impression that Jesus is being coerced into the Crucifixion by an arrogant will; rather, he is being asked to cooperate. His struggle is not that of a rebel against unreasonable authority, but rather that of human weakness against the inability to trust and the fear of death. He does not accept God's will with doomed resignation, but with free confidence. "Yet not what I will but what thou wilt," are words of triumph not defeat, of serenity not resignation. God's will is true, therefore death by it is life, despite the shrinking of the flesh. The

Resurrection reveals the content of God's Gethsemane will, the nature of an "Abba" to be trusted.

When Jesus gave his disciples a prayer, he was following the current custom. Teachers such as John the Baptist (Luke 11:1), for instance, would give their disciples a prayer in which they distilled the essence of their teaching. Jesus took a benediction from the synagogue liturgy as the foundation of his prayer. The "Kaddish" ended the sermon and was, therefore, an Aramaic rather than a Hebrew prayer; since, although the liturgy was in Hebrew, the sermon was in the vernacular Aramaic. It reads as follows:

> Glorified and sanctified be His great name in the world which He created according to His will. May His kingdom come in your lifetime and in your days, and in the lifetime of the whole house of Israel, soon and without delay. And to this say: "Amen."[32]

Jesus had known this prayer for the kingdom all his life; to it he added the phrases which defined his understanding of the nature of that kingdom, and at their head he placed the invocation "Abba."

The Lord's Prayer occurs in Matt. 6:9–13 and Luke 11:2–4. Under normal circumstances we would attribute a saying thus attested to the putative source Q, which is the source of much of the material common to Matthew and Luke. However, in this case the differences between the two versions are of a kind that suggests separate sources. The Lukan version is shorter and in that aspect nearer the original, since the tradition would not subtract material from so sacred a text. However, in a form like "debts" (Matt. 6:12) rather than "sins" (Luke 11:4) Matthew reflects the original Aramaic, in which the word for sin, *hoba,* is actually the term for a monetary debt.[33] Jeremias reconstructs the original as follows:

> Dear Father (Abba)
> May your name be hallowed,
> May your kingdom come,
> Give us today our bread for tomorrow
> And forgive us our debts
> As we also, herewith, forgive our debtors,
> And let us not fall into temptation.[34]

32. Jeremias, *ibid.,* 164.
33. *Ibid.,* 159.
34. *Ibid.,* 161.

The Matthean additions are for the sake of euphony and balance in the liturgy.

There are five petitions in the prayer, two in the second person singular and three in the plural. All are concerned with the kingdom: the first two are direct appeals for its establishment, the last two are requests concerning the conditions of entry, and the middle petition asks for a foretaste of the kingdom's future bliss. Since the content of a prayer is consonant with the nature of the divinity supplicated, we shall discover the nature of Jesus' "dear Father" by examining the requests made to him.

The first and most important request is taken from the Kaddish; that God's name may be glorified and held in honor by all people through the establishment of his sovereignty over the earth. The first two petitions are, therefore, synonymous and may be treated as one. "Sovereignty" or "rule" is a better translation of the Aramaic *malkutha* than "kingdom" because it avoids the implication of a special place.[35] We pray for the rule of God over all the world and not for the setting up of a separate place to which the righteous may flee from the world. Two things are implied by this petition; that the world in its present state is not as it should be; and that God in his sovereignty may be trusted.

Centuries of defeat and exile had convinced the Jews that the world in its present state was not as it should be. God had pledged himself to them, however, and sooner or later they would be vindicated. In the second century B.C., during the Maccabean resistance to the Syrian-Greek oppression, an anonymous author expressed this confidence in vivid images. In Daniel 7 the heathen oppressors appear as animal monsters, their ferine fury directed against the saints of God. The order of creation is upset and beasts rule over humankind (Gen. 1:28; 2:19–20). Then God asserts his power through a human agent, who with an appearance "like a son of man" governs the peoples on earth, at the head of the saints of God. Thus Adam rules the animals again, and creation is back in order. When a Jew prayed for the coming of the kingdom, he had Daniel 7 in mind; and, in the time of Jesus, he had the Roman eagle on his back to give urgency to his supplication. Jesus was

35. N. Perrin, *Rediscovering*, 55.

identified with the human agent of Daniel 7, and given the title "Son of Man." He seems to have accepted it as an appropriate sign of his identity.[36] God's sovereignty is not described; it is prayed for "sight unseen"; God is trusted. There is no alternative to trust, because the kingdom is for the future and "to see is no longer to hope" (Rom. 8:24). Nevertheless, there are grounds for hope in the glimpses of a good time to come which God gives in anticipation. "Abba" is a bright gleam of the dawning light, a ray from the new day. "Abba" recalls God's goodness, which promised land and posterity to the fathers, and liberated their children from slavery; God's patience which endured the pain of rejection, and by discipline and long-suffering sought reconciliation; God's faithfulness which can be relied on to vindicate the truth and elevate the just. "Abba" anticipates the triumph of God's goodness, patience and faithfulness in a time of true humanity under the sign of the Son of Man. "Abba" reveals Jesus to be the Son, in whom the fullness of God is present for us, and the reign of God revealed for our hope. Because the selfless humanity of Jesus did not end in defeat, but rather was affirmed by Resurrection, we know that such humanity is true; we too can risk living like that. "Abba" is the key to the identity and consciousness of Jesus, and Jesus is the human form of God as love.

The third petition, for the bread of tomorrow,[37] does not shift our attention from the horizons to the problems at hand, rather it maintains the tip-toe of expectation. In this plea we ask for a foretaste of the future to sustain our hope. The "bread of tomorrow" is the food of the Messianic banquet, the marriage feast of the lamb which we shall celebrate when God's kingdom comes. There is a note of accommodation here; if we cannot have the kingdom "soon and without delay," may we at least taste the substance of things hoped for. The eucharist is, therefore, both a grateful remembering of Christ's death, and a joyous anticipation of our new life, a symbolic sharing in the Resurrection. "Abba" signifies God's sustaining love in time of trial, as Jesus' Gethsemane experience shows. Our father

36. R. G. Hamerton-Kelly, *Pre-existence, Wisdom and the Son of Man* (Cambridge: University Press, 1973) .

37. See Jeremias, *Abba*, 165–6; *Theology*, 199, for a justification of this translation.

feeds us with the bread of heaven, nourishes our faith and keeps our hope alive (John 6). The third petition is a prayer for the provisional presence of God.

The plea for forgiveness does not stress the anger of God so much as the estrangement of men. The putative Aramaic makes clear that God's forgiveness of us is concomitant with our forgiveness of each other.[38] Behind the Greek of the second stanza lies an Aramaic perfect present which signifies an activity beginning here and now. So the translation, "as we, herewith, forgive others" is most accurate. The question which is of most interest to Protestant dogmatics, whether God's forgiveness is dependent on our willingness to forgive, is not entertained. This much is clear, however: there will be no divine forgiveness for those who harbor grudges. Jesus emphasizes this by breaking the symmetry of his prayer in order to add the proviso; he spoke of it on other occasions too (Mark 11:25; Matt. 5:23 ff.), and told a parable (Matt. 18:21–35) to bring home the importance of the fact that his "heavenly father" would not forgive us "unless you each forgive your brother from your hearts" (Matt. 18:35). The kingdom is a time of reconciliation and peace; as God acquits us in the final judgment so we drop all claims we have against each other, and thus the peace of God prevails. The plea for forgiveness is framed in the light of the final judgment which will precede the kingdom (Dan. 7:13 ff.), but we ask for it today as part of our ration of tomorrow's bread. So "Abba" means mutual forgiveness and reconciliation, marks of the community of the kingdom, of the church as a sign of the new society.

In this light the divisions in the church can only be evidence that we have fallen to the temptations from which we pray to be delivered in the final petition. The Greek which implies that God leads us to temptation is a misunderstanding of the Aramaic causative with permissive nuance which Jesus spoke.[39] Our translation, "and do not permit us to fall to temptation," is a plea to be sustained in the midst of the temptation which is bound to come, rather than a request to be kept from temptation altogether. This petition was also framed against the background of the events which were expected to precede the kingdom, in this case the suffering of the just

38. Jeremias, *Abba,* 159–160, 168.
39. *Ibid.,* 169.

in the final outburst of evil; and it also pertains to the present as the time when we may anticipate the end. Thus "Abba" in the last petition means support in time of trial, a sustenance for which the Christians found early need; and their need was met in the remembrance of "Abba."[40]

The Lord's Prayer reveals God the Father to be the one who moves history towards true humanity. He gives us a foretaste of that humanity in the experience of forgiveness and reconciliation, and in the sustenance that comes in times of temptation. Most of all, however, the prayer reveals Jesus to be the human face of God, for "Abba" is an address of deepest intimacy which only *the* son could use. In giving his disciples this prayer Jesus admitted them to the privilege of divine sonship and daughterhood, the right to call God "Abba" (cf. Rom. 8.15–16), and thereby bestowed on them the true humanity of the Kingdom of God.

The saying in Matt. 11:25–27 (=Luke 10:21–22) confirms and deepens our impression of the importance of the father symbol for Jesus' understanding of God. In this saying from Q, which begins as a prayer and turns into a pronouncement, we encounter the same primitive level of tradition as in the prayers of Jesus. It shows us that "Father" ("Abba") is the sign of the self-revelation of God through Jesus, the ground of Jesus' identity and authority. The prayer is as follows:

> I thank thee, Father, Lord of heaven and earth, for hiding these things from the learned and wise, and revealing them to the simple. Yes, Father, such was thy choice (Matt. 11:25–26 = Luke 10:21).

Behind "Father" lies the original "Abba," and the things which the simple see and the wise overlook are the things pertaining to Jesus, who he is and what he proclaims. These things are described in the following pronouncement:

> Everything is entrusted to me by my Father; and no one knows the son but the Father, and no one knows the Father but the son, and those to whom the son may choose to reveal him (Matt. 11:27 = Luke 10:22).

This saying, Semitic in form and content, has good grounds for being

---

40. Mark 14:36; Matt. 10:20; cf. Luke 12:12; cf. Sifra Lev. 20:26 (Jeremias, *Abba* 22) for a Jewish parallel to fatherly aid in persecution.

an authentic word of Jesus.[41] It contains a "hidden parable," as C. H. Dodd discovered.[42] The relationship between God and Jesus is like that between a father and a son; nobody understands a son like his father, and nobody understands a father like his son. The parable gains pungency from its social background: in Jesus' society a father initiated his son into the words of the Torah and into the secrets of his craft or trade. Whatever a father knew he passed on to his son, things he would not give to anyone else. Jesus claims to have received such a self-communication from God. In the technical language for the handing on of legal and religious tradition he claims, "Everything has been handed on to me by my father," just as in everyday life fathers reveal themselves and their skills to their sons. As a consequence, Jesus, the son, can reveal his father to those whom he chooses, and no one else can reveal the father in this way because no one else is the son.

The evidence suggests that Jesus observed certain distinctions between himself and his disciples on the one hand and between the disciples and those outside on the other, and that these are marked by the various forms of the "father" appellation. The phrase "my father," as we find in Matt. 11:27, marks an esoteric teaching for the disciples only—that is why they were chosen. To them Jesus entrusted the secret of his God-relationship (cf. Mark 4:11); to those outside everything was in parables (Luke 15:11–32). The other sayings in which Jesus addresses God as "my father" should be considered in the light of our Q saying (Matt. 11:25–27 = Luke 10:21–22); by a principle of analogy we might decide their authenticity. The prime and perhaps only candidate for such authentication is Matt. 16:17, where Peter's confession of Jesus as the Christ was revealed to him "by my heavenly father." It has the same "revelation" theme as our Q saying, and the same divine address. Luke 22:29, "now I vest in you the kingship which my father vested in me," may be authentic because of the revelation of the connection between Jesus and the

---

41. Jeremias, *Abba* 47–50; Paul Hoffman, *Studien zur Theologie der Logienquelle* (Münster: Aschendorff, 1972) 106 ff.; W. D. Davies, " 'Knowledge' in the Dead Sea Scrolls and Matthew 11:25–30," in *Christian Origins and Judaism* (Philadelphia: Westminster, 1962) 119–144.

42. Jeremias, *Abba* 50, quoting C. H. Dodd, "Une parabole cachée dans le quatrième Évangile," *Revue d'Histoire et de Philosophie Religieuses* 42 (1962) 107–115, cf. John 5:19–20a.

kingdom, and the confining of the revelation to the disciples. All the other "my father" attestations are secondary,[43] and must be treated as a part of the later traditions to which they belong. "My father" therefore is a mark of the self-revelation of Jesus; it is never reported that he shared with the disciples the address "our father" and we assume that in fact he never did. Just as the revelation of his identity to the disciples set them apart from the world so his consciousness of God as "Abba" set him apart from his disciples.

Jesus did, however, admit his disciples to this special God-relationship, albeit in a derivative mode. In addressing them he refers to God as "your father." We may note briefly some of the more significant sayings.[44] Mark 11:25,

> And when you stand praying, if you have a grievance against anyone, forgive him, so that your father in heaven may forgive you the wrongs you have done,

is clearly a fragment from the tradition of the Lord's Prayer. Mark includes it in a brief catechism on prayer (11:23–25), confirming that for Jesus and the early Christians the "father" title was especially at home in this context. The present form of the saying is probably an adaptation from the tradition of the Lord's Prayer. Luke 6:36 (= Matt. 5:48),[45] "Be compassionate as your father is compassionate," makes essentially the same point; that our forgiveness and God's are bound up with one another. Luke 12:30 (= Matt. 6:32), "but you have a father who knows that you need them," teaches confidence in prayer, as Luke 12:32, "Have no fear, little flock; for your father has chosen to give you the kingdom," casts out anxiety. "Your father," therefore, is Jesus' name for the God to whom his disciples should pray. He is a compassionate father who forgives us our trespasses and provides for our every need, especially our need for the fulfillment of our humanity in the kingdom. In the light of

---

43. Luke 2:49; 24:49; Matt. 7:21; 20:32; 12:50; 15:13; 18:10, 19, 35; 20:23; 25:34; 26:29, 53; Jeremias, *Abba* 46–47; we do not accept his argument that Mark 13:32 is a "my father" saying manqué, *ibid.*, 40.

44. The sayings in question are Mark 11:25; Q — Matt. 5:48 = Luke 6:36; Matt. 6:32 = Luke 12:30; Matt. 23:9; and Luke 12:32, in which Jesus, speaking to the disciples, calls God "your father." The other occurrences (Matt. 5:16, 45; 6:1, 14, 15, 26; 7:11; 10:20, 29; 18:14; 23:9; John 8:42; 20:17) are secondary (Jeremias, *Abba* 42–3).

45. The Lukan version is nearer the original, Jeremias, *ibid.*, 43.

this special significance of the address "Abba," it is understandable that Jesus should have forbidden his followers to call anyone on earth "Abba" (Matt. 23:9).[46] The prohibition was directed against the casual custom of calling older men "Abba" as a sign of respect. In ceasing to do this, the disciples showed that the address had special meaning for them. However, they would have demonstrated this all the more effectively if they had ceased to address their actual fathers in this way! The evidence that disciples experienced estrangement from their families or tensions in the family ties suggests that they might, indeed, have denied the title to their own fathers; but this must remain a conjecture.

The sayings on compassion and forgiveness which we have just considered are constructed on the idea that the things on earth should correspond to the things in heaven. In this case it is God's heavenly forgiveness and compassion that should be manifested on earth. Matthew, or his tradition, expressed the idea pungently when he added to the Lord's Prayer, "Thy will be done on earth as it is in heaven," after the petition for the kingdom (6:10). The idea is one of the foundation stones of apocalyptic thought; in Daniel (e.g. 7) and Revelation (e.g. 13), for instance, the triumph of the saints on earth is a manifestation of their triumph in heaven. Luke 11:13 (= Matt. 7:11) displays the same apocalyptic structure:

> If you, then, bad as you are, know how to give your children what is good for them, how much more will the heavenly Father give the Holy Spirit to those who ask him!

(Matthew's version [7:11] contains his well-known phrase "your heavenly Father," which, as we shall see, is a sign of the Matthean presence). The saying argues for the generosity of God from the kindness of earthly fathers, by the device "from the lesser to the greater." It is the same form of reasoning as in the "hidden parable" of Matt. 11:27 = Luke 10:22, and, indeed, in all the parables, namely, the analogy between heaven and earth. The tone of the saying suggests it was spoken to opponents who challenged Jesus' declaration of the goodness of God. In that case it is clear why he used "the Father" rather than "your Father." The final saying of this kind we shall consider, Mark 13:32 (cf. 8:38), was also probably

---

46. Jeremias, *ibid.*, 44–45 on the authenticity.

spoken to opponents, who asked for a specific time for the end of history as a corroboration of his authority. In refusing to give such information Jesus also used "the Father."

So Jesus used the appellation "Father" on three levels of intimacy: "My Father" when he prayed and when he revealed his identity as the son to his disciples; "your Father" when he taught his disciples how to pray to a God who cared for them with compassion and forgiveness, and assured them of a good time to come; "the Father" when defending his message against doubters and attack.

In comparison with the Judaism of his time, Jesus' teaching on the fatherhood of God is remarkable for its centrality in his theology, the intimacy of relationship which it signifies, and the relative reserve of the demand for obedience, so prominent in the Jewish sources. We are urged to imitate our father, to be compassionate and forgiving as he is, not commanded to do what he himself does not do. It is a case of "doing what he does, rather than what he merely says." God as "Abba" influences us by examples, and relates to us like a parent to children who have come of age. His promises are far more prominent than his demands; more than anything he desires to be intimately related to his children. This is nowhere more vividly evident than in the famous parable of the prodigal son, or, as it has also been called, the parable of the two sons (Luke 15:11–30). The parables are generally accepted as part of the teaching of the historical Jesus. In this parable Jesus sets forth the meaning of God's fatherhood for us: it is joyous acceptance without reference to deserts, when we freely return to him. He will not hold us by relations of necessity; we are free to take our goods and go into a far country. But when we freely return, he welcomes us with joy, and comes to meet us. "Abba" means that God is love; it is a repristination of the primordial experience of reality as good, expressed three thousand years before Christ in the hymn to the Moon God Sin from Ur: "Compassionate and merciful father in whose hand the life of the whole land lies"; to this Jeremias replies: "From the earliest time the word 'Father' when applied to God included for the Orientals something of what 'mother' means to us."[47] Jesus was such an "Oriental."

---

47. *Ibid.,* 162.

CHAPTER 4

God the Father

in the Earliest

Traditions about Jesus

We have already seen how Jesus' call to discipleship was muted by a church settling down to the long haul of history, when that call threatened the bonds of the patriarchal family. The new age began in, with, and under the forms of the old, giving rise to situations like that presented in 1 Corinthians 11, where Paul tries vainly to join together what God had put asunder, to hold the two ages together and to maintain both the right of a woman to speak in church (new) and the demand that she wear a veil (old). This eschatological tension was an essential part of the process, whose earliest stages are recorded in the New Testament, by which Christianity developed from its rudiments into a universal religion; but it was not the only part. The memory of the teaching of the historical Jesus played an equally important role in the process, and at the heart of that teaching is the figure of God the Father.

The traditions about Jesus in the New Testament are of different kinds: some focus on his words (Q), some on his deeds (Paul and Mark), and some combine a focus on words and deeds (Matthew, Luke, and John). None of them has a merely biographical interest; all seek to unpack the meaning of the confession that Jesus is the Christ of God. Therefore, the interest in his deeds concentrated initially on those which revealed his cosmic significance, on the Crucifixion and Resurrection as the events by which he achieved cosmic lordship, and the miracle stories which declared this dignity beforehand. The meaning of these events is always their meaning for us, for our salvation. The sayings occur within the frame of reference of these significant deeds, and whatever their original import might have been, we hear them now as the words of the risen Lord of history, rather than the sayings of a mere teacher from Nazareth. They speak of his significance for our salvation, and since the tradition remembers that "Abba" was the key to his conception of God, the idea of God as Father is central to the exposition. We shall consider the major instances in which the tradition expounds the meaning of Jesus' "Abba."

CHRISTIANS AS ADOPTED MEMBERS OF GOD'S FAMILY: THE APOSTLE PAUL

Paul gives us the earliest written account of how Jesus' Father-God was understood in Christian tradition. The writings of the apostle to the Gentiles pre-date the synoptic traditions (with the possible exception of Q) by between ten (Romans) and twenty (1 Thessalonians) years; but it is not their primitive character alone that makes the epistles so important. More significant than an early date is Paul's closeness to the theology of the historical Jesus, shown by the fact that he places the father image at the center of his doctrine of God's nature and work. He does this primarily by presenting the Christian life as membership by adoption in the family of God. The letters to the Galatians and to the Romans contain the most explicit statements of this theme.

In Galatians Paul tackles his major problem most resolutely: what are the theological grounds for his declaration that the law of Moses is passé? Apparently he had not made these clear to his Galatian converts, since they were turning to a form of Christianity which included obedience to the Mosaic law. Such recourse to Moses was an insult to Christ, suggesting that his power was not sufficient to forge and maintain their relationship with God. Furthermore, it was a submission to secondary divine powers and as such a humiliation comparable to that of the son of the house being under the authority of a household slave or other guardians, during his minority (Gal. 3:24; 4:3).

The stage of the argument that concerns us begins in Gal. 3:15 and ends at 4:11. In scripture God promised Abraham a posterity ("seed"—singular); by license of rabbinic exegesis Paul takes the fact that "seed" is singular and not plural to mean that scripture had only one descendant in mind, namely, Jesus. This heir was given to Abraham by God's promise and not in return for his obedience to the Mosaic law, which in any case was promulgated 430 years later than the promise and so could in no way affect it. Paul then talks about "the inheritance" (v. 18) which had likewise been given by promise and not earned. The heir (Christ) and the inheritance (the blessing) merge in the statement:

> For through faith you are all sons of God in union with Christ Jesus. Baptized into union with him you have all put on Christ as a garment. There is no such thing as Jew and Greek, slave and freeman, male and female; for you are all one person in Christ Jesus. But if you thus belong to Christ, you are the 'issue' of Abraham, and so heirs by promise (vv. 26–29).

Those who believe in Christ are the blessed offspring of Abraham and so within the orbit of God's promised grace. It is not necessary to seek legislated grace from Moses. Thus Paul sought to settle the uncertainties of those who wanted to add Mosaic obedience to Christian faith.

The metaphor of Abraham's "offspring" which culminated in the assurance that all believers in Christ are God's children because they have identified themselves with the heir of the blessing promised to Abraham, leads on to more detailed imagery. In 4:1–7 the fundamental metaphor is that of the children of God; before the advent of Christ, relationship to God by faith was not possible; only by obedience to Moses' law could one be numbered among God's children (Israel was God's adopted family—Rom. 9:4; cf. Exod. 4:22). That state was comparable to a minor heir who, although he owns everything, is under the authority of trustees until he attains the age declared by his father for entering upon his inheritance. In such subordination the heir is no better off than a slave, even though he is in fact an heir, and such were those under Mosaic obedience before Christ made faith possible and set them free to act like sons rather than slaves.

> To prove that you are sons, God has sent into our hearts the Spirit of his Son, crying, "Abba! Father!" You are therefore no longer a slave but a son, and if a son, then also by God's own act an heir (4:6–7; cf. Rom. 8:12–17).

Thus Paul's exposition, which begins with Abraham the father of all who believe, culminates in Jesus' invocation of God, as the father of all who by faith have united themselves with Jesus.

As elsewhere in Paul (e.g. Rom. 7:1–6), the metaphor is not symmetrical. It begins with the principals as minor sons who have only to attain their majority, and shifts to the image of slaves whose freedom is purchased and who are then adopted as sons (4:5). What should have been a declaration of maturity is in fact an adoption. Lietzmann suggests that Paul made this change because he realized that Gentiles did not have the residual sense of sonship which Jews would have had[1] and so for them the experience would have been more like adoption than coming of age. If we are to have an explanation at all, this seems as good as any; but it does not change the fact that the apostle is, once again, rather careless in his use of imagery.

The custom of purchasing a slave with a view to adoption is not widely attested in the Roman world of the time. Even rarer are the cases of manumission by adoption; Justinian attributes to Cato the rule that a master could liberate his own slave by adoption, and Aulus Gellius observes, as of antiquarian interest, that at one time a master could give his slave in adoption.[2] In any case, while the evidence for a well-established connection between manumission and adoption is slender in the Greco-Roman world, the image of the Exodus as an adoption subsequent to liberation is powerfully present in Paul's biblical heritage (Exod. 6:7). The change in imagery, therefore, may be due to the influence of the Exodus on Paul's thought rather than to his awareness that the Gentiles had no sense of residual sonship like the Jews and so would find the symbol of adoption more striking than the declaration of maturity.

If this is so we have two images of a relationship freely joined rather than determined by law or nature. A minor is bound by law to his father's will and cannot exercise a responsible stewardship in his father's house. His relationship to the father is one of dependence and subservience. When he comes of age, however, the legal bonds dissolve and he is free to enter into a responsible relationship with his father based on mutual recognition and taking the form of adult reciprocity. A slave is similarly without responsibility and so in infantile dependency; when he becomes an adopted son (as Israel

1. *An die Galater* (Tübingen: Mohr, 1932).
2. W. W. Buckland, *The Roman Law of Slavery from Augustus to Justinian* (Cambridge: University, 1908, reprinted 1970) 448; S. Scott Bartschy, *First-century Slavery and 1 Corinthians 7:21*, SBL Diss. Series 11 (Missoula: S.B.L. 1973).

did in the Exodus) he enters a freely chosen relationship. Thus a legal and a natural relationship is broken and restored on a new level of freedom and respect, as in Ricoeur's version of the negotiation of the Oedipus complex. We are God's adult children, says Paul, not his slaves or his babies; faith is a mature relationship to God, like that of adults to their parents.

The contrast of slavery and sonship in association with the "Abba" exclamation and a reference to the Spirit also occurs in Rom. 8:12–17. Käsemann[3] takes the phrase "moved by the Spirit" (NEB)[4] in v. 14 to indicate that Paul had a situation of ecstatic worship in mind as he composed these lines (cf. 1 Cor. 12:2). The cry "Abba, Father" was an ecstatic acclamation in early Christian worship, made with special meaning by the newly baptized, but in general use in worship as well. Early Christian worship seems to have favored such Aramaic exclamations: "Amen" occurs frequently in liturgical material[5] and "Maranatha" (Our Lord come!) is attested once.[6] There is, however, no reason to oppose liturgical tradition to the tradition of the teaching of Jesus, as Käsemann does. It is likely that significant fragments of the latter would find their way into the former, especially Aramaic words which would have carried the sort of mysterious authority—for Greek speakers—which liturgy, of an ecstatic kind, might favor. In addition to these general speculations we might consider that the three words in question are also connected with pivotal points in the teaching of Jesus and are therefore prime candidates to be remembered: "Abba" with the conception of God; "Amen" with the veracity of Jesus' utterances;[7] and "Maranatha" with the prayer for the kingdom, which is the kernel of the Lord's Prayer. Therefore, we have a good example in our text of how the Jesus tradition was used in worship. In Gal. 4:6 the Spirit who provokes the "Abba" cry is called "the Spirit of his Son"; in Rom. 8:15 he is "the Spirit of adoption" ("the Spirit who makes us sons"— NEB). The form and content of these verses is so similar that we

---

3. *An die Römer,* 3 Aufl. (Tübingen: Mohr, 1974).

4. Literally, "driven by the Spirit."

5. Rom. 1:25; 9:5; 11:36; 15:33; 16:24, 27; 1 Cor. 14:16; 16:24, etc.

6. 1 Cor. 16:22.

7. Note how characteristically he used it as an asseveration: "Truly, truly (Amen, Amen) I say to you."

are safe in assuming that Paul is using the same formula in each. Therefore we may regard the two descriptions of the Spirit as equivalent: the Spirit of God's Son is the Spirit of adoption; we become God's adopted children by uniting ourselves with Christ through faith. The primitive conception of how the Spirit operates, which was current in Paul's milieu, held that the "Abba" exclamation was a sign of this union with Christ. Just as Jesus called God "Abba" and revealed thereby his divine sonship, so do Jesus' disciples.

As was his custom, Paul meets his readers where they are; he uses their own understanding of things in order to make his point. His point is that the relationship with God which Jesus makes possible is free from slavish fear, full of adult confidence—that their own uninhibited Spirit-cry "Abba!" is evidence of this (v. 15). If, however, some believed that this Spirit identified them totally with Christ, here and now, so that they are already saved, Paul warns that they are mistaken: we are God's heirs, but only as Christ's fellow-heirs, and as he suffered in this age so must we, if we are to share in the inheritance with him later (v. 17). "For we have been saved, though only in hope" (v. 24). So we see that the apostle, although he uses material from a context of ecstatic worship, is soberly critical of excessive enthusiasm, especially of the kind that loses touch with the reality of struggle in this world. We also see that the "Abba" tradition was at home in worship; and this is not surprising, because the Jesus tradition tells us that "Abba" was the heart of Jesus' own worship.

Indeed, the Pauline evidence suggests that the father appellation was confined to liturgical and quasi-liturgical usage. The early Christians did not talk *about* God as father, they talked *with* him. There is a broad spectrum of such liturgical utterances in the Epistles, and many of them contain material that was the common heritage of the church. Paul begins all his Epistles with the invocation, "Grace and Peace from God the Father and the Lord Jesus Christ" (Rom. 1:7; 1 Cor. 1:3; 2 Cor. 1:2; Gal. 1:3–4; Phil. 1:2; 1 Thess. 1:1; Philemon 3), an indication that the knowledge of God's fatherhood is given in connection with Jesus Christ. Furthermore the appellation occurs in a thanksgiving (2 Cor. 1:3; 1 Thess. 1:2–3), an oath (2 Cor. 11:31), an acclamation (Phil. 2:11; 4:20), an intercession (1 Thess. 3:11–13), a benediction (Rom. 15:6; 2 Thess. 2:16–17), a baptismal liturgy (Rom. 6:4), and a creed (1 Cor. 8:6; 15:24). When we add to these the acclamations in Gal. 4:6–7 and Rom. 8:14–17, which we have already discussed, the evidence for a liturgical context appears to be conclusive.

God the Father, therefore, was the living reality of early Christian experience, the appellation by which that experience was focused and celebrated in public worship and private prayer. We may recall, with renewed appreciation, Jeremias' judgment that the gift which Jesus gave his disciples was the privilege of sharing in his own filial relationship to God, which was the mature relationship of a child come of age. Paul shows that the church cherished this privilege in its worship. He gives expression to it in his own words when he calls the Spirit which animates that worship, "the Spirit of his Son," and "the Spirit of adoption," received in union with Christ through faith.[8]

THE CHURCH AS THE
UNITED FAMILY OF GOD: MATTHEW

Recent scholarship acknowledges that the evangelists were as much interpreters of Jesus, each with his own theological emphasis, as was the apostle Paul. This is clearly evident in the case of the fourth evangelist, John, and has long been recognized. In the case of the synoptic evangelists, Matthew, Mark, and Luke, however, the realization has dawned relatively late. They were regarded as biographers of Jesus in the earlier stages of modern scholarship, and, when that view was shown to be mistaken, became in the reaction vestigial presences. The synoptic Gospels were seen as the deposit of communal tradition, molded by anonymous forces whose nature was accessible only by folkloristic methods. "The tradition" became the

8. For the sake of completeness we may notice that Paul refers to himself as the "father" of his congregations (1 Cor. 4:15; 2 Cor. 6:13; 11:2–3; 12:14; Gal. 4:19; 1 Thess. 2:11) and as "father" of certain individuals (Phil. 2:22; Philemon 10). On both the Rabbinic and the Hellenistic side of early Christianity there is precedent for such usage. Resh Lachish (A.D. 250) said: "Whoever teaches his neighbor's son Torah, the Scripture regards as if he had conceived him" (Sanh. 99[b] in *Str-B* III, 341, cf. *Str-B* II, 559). On the Hellenistic side, in the mysteries the mystagogue, who initiates the postulants, is called their father, and in a more general usage the notion of spiritual fatherhood is present (H. Conzelmann, *1 Corinthians, A Commentary on the First Epistle to the Corinthians,* Hermeneia Series [Philadelphia, Fortress, 1975] 91).

creative matrix from which the Gospels emerged by a quasi-natural labor. One pioneer of this approach, Rudolf Bultmann, described it as the application of sociology to biblical study. Now, however, a more balanced view prevails which takes into account both the communal nature of the tradition and the contribution of the individual evangelist. According to this view the evangelists recorded the tradition with a theological purpose of their own and this purpose can be discerned in the way they organized the received material and in the additions and omissions which they made.

Of the three synoptic Gospels, Matthew presents the most vivid interpretation of the father idea. There is a marked increase in the occurrence of the term by comparison with Mark and Luke, and we have seven sayings in which Matthew has the term "father" while Luke, in reporting the same logia, does not. In view of the general situation, it seems probable that Luke contains a more original form of these sayings and that "father" was added by Matthew.[9] "Father," therefore, was of special importance to him.

Jeremias thinks that this added importance occurred in the Matthean tradition before the evangelist received it. There were special factors at work in Matthew's community which brought this about. There was an increase in the popularity of the term in the Judaism to which his church was exposed, as a result of the favor which the influential Rabbi Johanan ben Zakkai bestowed on it; Christian prophets who favored it were especially active in that church; and it played a significant role in catechesis and liturgy, both special interests of Matthew's tradition.[10] It is not important for our purpose to maintain a clear distinction between the evangelist and his tradition, and so we shall treat "the evangelist Matthew" as a name for the Gospel and its tradition.

Matthew contains three clusters of "Father" references which are unparalleled: a catechesis on prayer (6:1–18); a catechesis on conduct in the church (18:10–35); and a missionary charge, especially advice on how to endure under persecution (10:16–32). The first two clusters are characteristically Matthean reflections on themes from

---

9. They are Matt. 5:45 = Luke 6:35; Matt. 6:26 = Luke 12:24; Matt. 7:21 = Luke 6:46; Matt. 10:20 = Luke 12:12; Matt. 10:29 = Luke 12:6; Matt. 10:32 = Luke 12:8; Matt. 18:14 = Luke 15:7.

10. Jeremias, *Abba*, 37.

the Lord's Prayer, especially the petition for forgiveness as we forgive others. Matthew frequently uses the words or deeds of Jesus as
a basis for theological reflection in the style of contemporaneous
rabbinic exposition. The Jesus tradition was for him a holy word
whose implications had to be drawn out, much as the commentaries
of the rabbis, called Midrash and Gemara, did for the Jewish tradition of the time.

The center of the catechesis on prayer in 6:1–18 is, of course, the
Lord's Prayer itself (vv. 9–13). There are three parts: on good deeds
(1–4), on the right way to pray (5–14), and on the proper way to fast
(16–18). These subjects belong together in a teaching on prayer because they all affect the readiness with which our petitions are
received by God. Each section contains the admonition not to perform these pieties ostentatiously but rather in secret because "your
father who sees in secret" rewards such acts (vv. 4, 6, 18). Furthermore, we are to pray succinctly, in modest faith, because "your
father knows what your needs are before you ask him" (v. 8); and,
finally, we must forgive one another if we are to be forgiven by our
heavenly Father (v. 15). Thus we are told explicitly something of
what it means to share the privilege of praying the Lord's Prayer.
Invoking God as "Abba" entails modesty, humble trust, and mutual
forbearance. It is not hard to imagine the circumstances which made
such teaching necessary. Ostentation, verbosity, and vindictiveness
inevitably distort human community and they were surely not absent from the early Christian church. To counteract these distortions
Matthew expounds the "Abba" of Jesus' prayer; God is a Father who
rewards the modest, hears those of few words, and only forgives us
when we are forgiving towards others.

The cluster of "Father" sayings in chapter 18 addresses the same
situation, with particular attention to the possibility that weaker
members of the community might be scandalized by this self-asser-
tion and alienated from the gospel. The chapter begins with the
question, "Who is the greatest in the kingdom of heaven?" reflecting the rivalry present in the congregation. V. 10 introduces the
parable of the lost sheep with the warning never to "despise one of
these little ones" whose guardian angels in heaven "look continually
on the face of my heavenly father"; the parable is then presented as
a statement of the fact that God cares most for the little members

of the congregation. This can be seen in the fact that, instead of Luke's conclusion, "there will be greater joy in heaven over one sinner who repents" (Luke 15:7) which makes it an encouragement to mission, Matthew gives the parable a conclusion which makes it a warning against behavior which may cause the weak to leave the church: "In the same way it is not your father's will that one of these little ones should be lost" (Matt. 18:14; cf. v. 6). As the chapter began with the question, "Who is the greatest in the kingdom of heaven?" so it ends with the parable of the unforgiving servant and the warning,

> And so angry was the master that he condemned the man to torture until he should pay the debt in full. And that is how my heavenly Father will deal with you, unless you each forgive your brother from your hearts (18:34–35).

This is clearly a reminiscence of the Lord's Prayer, like 6:14 in the previous cluster, and its repetition shows that vindictiveness was a particular problem in Matthew's community. Thus "Father" is a symbol which calls for unity in the church based on the fact that this heavenly Father cares for his family, and especially for its weaker members.

By now it is apparent that the "Father" appellation occurred predominantly in the same situation for both Matthew and Paul, namely worship and the communal life of the church. Paul used the experience of God's fatherhood in worship as a basis for his argument that Christians need not lead a life of fear-inducing obedience to divine law, but could rather live in the freedom of a mature relationship with God. Matthew used the same experience to combat competitiveness and cement the unity of the church. The early Christians shared the filial consciousness of Jesus by virtue of their conviction that he had risen from the dead and was spiritually present to them, especially when they met for worship. In the congregations which Paul addresses, the presence of the risen Christ was called "the Spirit of his Son" (Gal. 4:6) or "the Spirit of adoption" (Rom. 8:15). Thus worship was a participation in the filial consciousness of Jesus.

In the Matthean missionary charge, we find the same idea of the Spirit entering the believer, in this case to provide emergency support for the persecuted. When they are summoned to answer before hostile tribunals, Christian missionaries need not worry about their defence; "when the time comes, the words you need will be given you; for it is not you who will be speaking: it will be the Spirit of your Father speaking in you" (10:20). The "Spirit of your Father" occurs only in Matthew's version of this Q saying: Luke has "the Holy Spirit" (Luke 12:12). Under normal circumstances we would judge Matthew's version to be more primitive because "Holy Spirit" is a technical term in later theology and a favorite with Luke. However, such a conclusion is not possible here because of Matthew's tendency to add "Father" to Q sayings, and the fact that the other "Father" sayings in our section of chapter 10 are both Q logia to which Matthew has made the addition. Whatever their original form might have been, Matthew intends the three sayings (10:20, 29 and 32–33) to express what it means to have a "Father-God."

On the one hand it means special support in time of need (10:20) and the assurance of God's providential care, not only for creation as a whole but also for individuals (10:29; cf. Luke 12:6). On the other hand it demands a fearless witness to the Son; those who do not acknowledge him before the world, he will not acknowledge before his heavenly Father (10:32–3; cf. Luke 12:8–9). Complete participation in Christ's sonship, expressed here as his acknowledging us brother or sister before his Father, depends, therefore, on our willingness to share Christ's earthly lot (10:24–5; cf. Rom. 8:17–18). Divine fatherhood is a promise and a present reality, "for we have been saved, though only in hope" (Rom. 8:24).

These notes of present caring and future blessing are sounded elsewhere by the Matthean "Father" sayings. Our good deeds proclaim the goodness of our heavenly Father (5:16), especially love for our enemies (5:45), which proves the impartial generosity of his paternal love, and his limitless goodness (5:48). As he cares for the birds of the air, so he cares for us (6:26). However, this love is not undiscriminating; God does not reward all, the just and the unjust, without distinction. On the contrary, his rewards are contingent on our response (6:1, 4, 18); only those who do the Father's will shall enter his kingdom (7:21); only those who acknowledge the Son will be acknowledged (10:32–33); only those who do the Father's will are Christ's brothers (12:50; cf. Mark 3:35). The righteous shall "shine as brightly as the sun in the kingdom of their Father" (13:43), a kingdom which has been prepared "from the foundation of the world" (25:34) as an expression of the Father's blessing. The Father controls absolutely who shall and shall not find entrance (15:13; 20:23), for it is his kingdom alone (26:29). Therefore, the Father's inclusive love intends to make all people righteous, not to erase the distinction between justice and injustice.

So, for Matthew, Father is the reality of the experience of worship, of community, of providence, and of eternal life. Christian confidence in the present and the future, which we celebrate in worship and attest by the quality of Christian community, rests on Jesus' revelation of the fatherhood of God.

THE CHRISTIAN COMMUNITY UNITED
AS THE FATHER AND THE SON ARE UNITED:
THE FOURTH GOSPEL

Matthew shows signs of having been composed in part as an exposition of the teaching of Jesus. The clusters we examined in chapter 6 and chapter 18 were both explanations of the practical meaning of elements from the Lord's Prayer. The Fourth Gospel is a more obvious example of the same procedure, excepting that it expounds the meaning of significant deeds rather than significant words of Jesus. It is composed on the basis of seven signs or miracle stories:[11] the turning of the water into wine (chap. 2); the healing of the officer's son (chap. 4); the healing of the lame man (chap. 5); the feeding of the multitude and the walking on the water (chap. 6); the healing of the blind man (chap. 9); and the raising of Lazarus (chap. 11). Long discourses occur in more or less close connection with these narratives,[12] and John clearly intends to show that the words of Jesus arise out of his deeds and that the deeds give rise to significant words.

The discourses are reminiscent of Hellenistic mystical religion: the farewell discourses in chapters 14–17 for instance recall texts from the *Corpus Hermeticum,* writings from a religion of Hellen-

---

11. C. H. Dodd, *The Interpretation of the Fourth Gospel* (Cambridge: University, 1960) 297 ff.

12. It is not possible to display a tidy relationship between narrative and discourse without rearranging the text too much; nevertheless the events and the discourses are linked sufficiently to support our judgment.

istic Egypt in New Testament times.[13] Jesus is a revealer, like Hermes, who begins the revelation in dialogue with the initiates (disciples) and then changes to a monologue and finally to a prayer (or hymn) in which the union of the revealer with his god is actualized. This is a general account of the process from chapter 14 where Jesus is in dialogue to chapter 17 where he prays in terms of the most intimate union with his father.

Unlike this Hellenistic religion, however, whose literary form the Fourth Gospel resembles in these chapters, the words of union are based on deeds of union. The request with which the climactic prayer in chapter 17 begins, "Glorify thy Son, that thy Son may glorify thee," refers to the Crucifixion and Resurrection. "Glorify" is a Johannine code word for the passion and Resurrection (cf. 12:23, 27–28), which, in this verse, indicates that the whole discourse (chaps. 14–17) finds its warrant in the following passion narrative (chaps. 18–21). This means that the unity for which chapter 17 prays—the unity of believers with Christ and therefore with one another—is the actualization of a possibility opened up by the death and Resurrection of Jesus. The passion was an event of unity between God and man; unity happened and from that happening there goes out into human history an energy that unites. John calls it "glory":

> . . . may they all be one: as thou, Father, art in me, and I in thee, so also may they be in us, that the world may believe that thou didst send me. *The glory which thou gavest me I have given them, that they may be one as we are one;* I in them and thou in me, may they be perfectly one (17:21–23).

"Glory" is Jesus' unity with the Father, which was demonstrated most clearly in his obedient trusting on the cross and his vindication on the third day. This "glory" we beheld in Jesus "full of grace and truth" (1:14), in his deeds (2:11), in his words (12:49–50; 6:68; 7:46; 3:31–34), and especially in his death and Resurrection; and we are united by it while we abide in Christ (15:1–4).

Thus we pick up again that strand of the "Father" tradition which leads through Matthew and Paul back to Jesus himself; namely, that God's fatherhood means union with one another through union with Christ. Jesus gave his disciples a prayer in which they addressed

God by the name which Jesus himself used, "Abba." In this way he admitted them to a share in his own relationship with God. This relationship was vindicated in Christ's Resurrection and made into an energy which shapes history. The nature of this energy is to form the family of God with Christ as the elder brother (Paul), to foster a united community in which there is no petty competitiveness (Matthew), to fill people with common life and so to make them all one, as the Son and the Father are one (John).

The Fourth Gospel concentrates on the doctrine of Christ with unparalleled intensity. "Father" is the predominant name for God because Jesus is preeminently the "Son." If Matthew shows an increase in the use of the term "Father" for God, John displays a veritable explosion of its popularity. This is because of his burning interest in "the Son." The opening dialogue in the farewell discourses states John's theme: "I am the way; I am the truth and the life; no one comes to the Father except by me. *If you knew me you would know the Father too . . . I am in the Father, and the Father in me*" (14:6, 7, 10), a theme which occurs again and again (e.g. 1:14, 18; 3:35–36; 8:16–19; 13:1).

Its most extended exposition, next to chapter 17, occurs in chapter 5. After healing the lame man at Bethesda pool on the Sabbath, Jesus has to defend his transgression of the Sabbath law. This he does by claiming: " 'My father has never yet ceased his work, and I am working too.' This made the Jews still more determined to kill him, because he was not only breaking the Sabbath, but, *by calling God his own Father, he claimed equality with God*" (5:17–18). In the discourse which follows we hear that the works of the Son are the works of the Father, since the Son copies the Father as a youngster who is being initiated into a trade by his father follows what his father does. C. H. Dodd sees a hidden parable here (5:19–20) like the one concealed in the Q saying (Matt. 11:27 = Luke 10:22) which we considered in our study of the teaching of Jesus.[14] The Father has given the Son the authority to judge and even the power to raise the dead (5:21, 16), of which it was said by Rabbi Johanan (Taanith 2a):

> Three keys are in God's hand which are given into the hand of no representative, namely the key of the rain (Deut. 28:12), the key of

14. "Une parable cachée."

the womb (Gen. 30:22), and the key of the resurrection of the dead (Ezek. 37:13).[15]

The form of relationship between the Father and the Son is that of the relationship between God and the prophets whom he sends; the content, however, is unique in the degree of unity of will between the sender and the one sent (5:30). "Father," therefore, is a symbol of Christ's status—as the Son.

Paradoxically this status is secured not by emphasizing the Son's equality with the Father but rather his dependence on the Father. He lives because of the Father (6:57), does only what he sees the Father doing (5:17 ff.), works miracles in the consciousness of an uninterrupted dependence on the Father (11:40–43), and speaks only what the Father instructs him to utter (12:49–50). This will be clearly seen in the passion:

> They did not understand that he was speaking to them about the Father. So Jesus said to them: "When you have lifted up the Son of Man you will know that I am what I am. I do nothing on my own authority, but in all that I say, I have been taught by my Father. He who sent me is present with me, and has not left me alone; for I always do what is acceptable to him" (8:27–30).

Thus John tells us that we might have confidence in Jesus' words and deeds; they are, indeed, truth and life because they are the words and deeds of God.

Finally, there are hints in the Fourth Gospel of a worship-context for the father image. In chapter 4 a discussion on the proper way to worship God is presented in the form of a discussion between Jesus and a woman of Samaria. They discuss the relative merits of the Jewish and Samaritan claims about the most holy place, whether it is Jerusalem, as the Jews aver, or Mount Gerizim, as the Samaritans hold. The conclusion is that ". . . the time approaches, indeed it is already here, when those who are real worshippers will worship the Father in spirit and in truth" (4:23). Chapter 17, which is one of the keys to the Gospel's understanding of the fatherhood of God, has the form of a prayer, indeed, is analogous to the hymn of unification with the deity, which effects salvation according to the Hermetic religion. So we may conclude that the idea of God as Father

---

15. C. K. Barrett, *The Gospel according to St. John, An Introduction with Commentary and Notes on the Greek text* (London: SPCK, 1972) 216.

had its place in the worship of the Johannine community, as in Paul's and Matthew's traditions.

THE "PROMISE TO THE FATHERS": LUKE–ACTS

Luke's particular contribution to our reflection is a repristination of the idea of "the fathers," which was so important in our discussion of the Old Testament evidence. The "fathers" were one of the marks by which Yahweh was identified; not only was his name "Yahweh"; not only was he the one who brought them out of Egypt; he was also the one who had entered into a special relationship with Abraham, Isaac and Jacob—he was "the God of the fathers" (cf. Acts 24:14). Once again the Deuteronomic theme of the "promise to the fathers" is a dominant note in the presentation of the nature of salvation (Luke 1:55, 72, 73; Acts 3:13; 5:30; 7:9, 30, 38). Luke–Acts views salvation as the hidden, spiritual dimension of history, and so is careful to connect the event of salvation in Jesus with its historical origin in the covenant with the fathers. Salvation takes place as history, and this can be seen from the course of history itself, when viewed as a whole from its origin to its end. Its origin lies in God's promise to the fathers, and its end is the fulfillment of that promise by the Resurrection of Jesus (Acts 13:32–33). Thus Jesus is the key to history's meaning; his Resurrection is a revelation of the fact that all things will, in the end, enter upon the resurrection form of life over which death has no power.

The history of Israel is not a simple story of fulfilled promise, however, it is also the story of resistance to God's desires, a chronicle of human wilfulness.

> How stubborn you are, heathen still at heart and deaf to the truth! You always fight against the Holy Spirit. Like fathers, like sons. Was there ever a prophet whom your fathers did not persecute? They killed those who foretold the coming of the Righteous One; and now you have betrayed him and murdered him, you who received the Law as God's angels gave it to you, and yet have not kept it (Acts 7:51–53).

So "fathers" becomes for the Christians a sign not only of salvation but also of rejection; and this is to be expected, because Judaism for the most part rejected Jesus and his movement out of loyalty to the "fathers." Christianity has therefore to attach itself to the "fathers" dialectically, saying both yes and no; yes, to the blessing given the world in Abraham and opened up for all through Jesus; no, to the preconceived notions which rejected Jesus because he did not fit their form of expectation, and no to the exclusivism which hoarded the blessing for the physical descendants of Abraham and the observers of Moses' law. Thus the past and the future are brought together without one becoming the prisoner of the other. The future affirms the relevance of some parts of the past and denies the relevance of others; the past enables us to understand those parts of the future which are significant, either as fulfillment or as denial of the promise which comes to us out of the past.

Luke–Acts was not alone in recognizing the importance of "the fathers" for an understanding of Jesus. Indeed, "the fathers" were a major theme amongst the theological concepts common to the early church. Paul makes much of the fathers as the bearers of the promise (Rom. 4:1, 11, 12, 17 ff.; 9:5, 11; 11:28; 1 Cor. 10:1; Gal. 3:7 ff.; 4:28) and for him, too, Christ is the fulfillment of God's promise to the fathers (Rom. 15:8). He even tries to express the dialectical relationship which Christianity found necessary. Instead of the tension between yes and no, Paul gives us a yes and a no clearly separate from each other. He has resolved the ambivalence by identifying yes with the promise and no with the law. That this solution raises as many questions as it seeks to answer cannot concern us here; all we want to establish is that Paul shared the idea of the "fathers" which became so prominent for Luke.

The negative evaluation of "the fathers" which we noticed in Luke–Acts also occurs in Q. In Q such condemnation is directed against those who believe that physical descent from "the fathers" will save them from condemnation by God for their injustice (Matt. 3:9 = Luke 3:8). It was believed that the merits of the fathers prevailed for their descendants in the judgment; hence it was important to be able to prove one's genealogy—a situation of genealogy instead of morals. Indeed, so important was this genealogical link that proselytes, who had no such connection, could not take advantage of the accumulated merits of the fathers.[16] Such doctrine was roundly condemned in Q, and the whole notion of "the fathers"

16. Foerster, *Zeitgeschichte*, 97–8.

was evaluated rather negatively (Matt. 23:32 = Luke 11:47; cf. Matt. 5:12 = Luke 6:26).

The earliest tradition shows a remarkable unanimity in interpreting the meaning of Jesus' teaching about the fatherhood of God. It entails that the believers are one family in union with Jesus the Son. Paul emphasizes the themes of adoption and freedom; we enter the family as mature adults, by the free choice of faith, and live in adult responsibility, not in infantile obedience. Matthew insists that the unity of the family be free of all competitiveness, and marked by humility and mutual caring, while John focuses on the divine source of the family's unity in the "glory" which binds the Father and the Son together and which is given to the believers to share. The sphere of worship is the context in which the fatherhood of God is most characteristically celebrated, and the unity of the Christian family experienced. Finally, reaching back behind the teaching of Jesus, Luke–Acts, Paul, and Q also reflect, albeit dialectically, on the Yahwistic theme of the "fathers" as the bearers of God's presence.

CHAPTER 5

Summary and Conclusion

We set out to discover the meaning of the symbol "father" used for God in the teaching of Jesus, viewing that teaching against its background in the Old Testament and Judaism, and across its foreground in the tradition of the early church. Because "father" is a symbol and so has at least two levels of meaning, we took Freud's Oedipus complex as the hypothetical content of the surface meaning and tested it against the historical evidence, regarded as the deep meaning, in order to see whether they illuminated one another. The time has come to ask whether the Oedipus hypothesis enabled us to see meaning in the history which would otherwise have remained hidden, and whether the history in turn suggests modifications in the hypothesis.

There is a remarkable unanimity throughout the biblical traditions in the understanding of what aspects of history the father symbol illuminates. At the level of indirect symbolization, "father" as applied to the divine revelation means liberation. It first occurs in the Mosaic traditions as a way of describing what God had done in liberating his people from Egyptian bondage. He had "adopted" them as his people (Exod. 6:6–8) and made them his "first-born son" (Exod. 4:23). By means of the idea of adoption any hint of a natural relationship between God and Israel, father and son, is expunged, and replaced by the idea of a free and gracious choice; election shows that the bonds of fate are broken and a new relationship based on free reciprocity established. So "father" means freedom in two senses: freedom from human bondage, and the freedom for a loving relationship with God based on faith rather than fate.

In order to experience this freedom of faith, the old order in which one's relationship with God depended on one's natural membership in the family, through whose patriarch God's presence was mediated, had to be changed. Abraham experienced God as the one who called him to go out into the world rather than to stay at home; only as he departed the graves of his ancestors did he experience the presence of God. Likewise in the cases of the endangered son (Isaac), the jeopardized wife (Sarah and Rebecca), the lost son (Joseph), God's grace was experienced through the breaking of the natural ties of family. Later, in prophetic times, the possibility of God's grace in the present was celebrated by identifying with the fathers who had experienced the liberation of the Exodus and had received the promise of the land; thus "fathers" became the symbol of God's liberating activity in history.

At the level of direct symbolization, the prophets used the father symbol—now a less firm male image than before, and apt to take on the characteristics of "mother" from time to time—as a foil for their indictments of Israel's sin and as a basis for the people's plea for forgiveness. It invokes the whole experience of God's saving activity on behalf of his people, a record for which they should be grateful, and which, therefore, proclaims the perversity of their unfaithfulness.

Jesus stands firmly in the tradition of the Exodus understanding that God's fatherhood means liberation, a release from earthly bondage and from a fated rather than a free relationship with God. In the name of the sovereignty of God, which he defined most explicitly as the exercise of God's fatherhood, he called people away from the bondage of natural family relationships to a new family joined by faith in God freely given. In his summons to discipleship and in the way he treated women, Jesus showed that kinship in the Kingdom of God was different from the patriarchy. Indeed, it is probable that his relatively free association with women was prominent among the contraventions of religious law and custom for which he was finally done to death.

This is not to say that he promulgated a program for the abolition of the nuclear family; whether he did or not we do not know; it seems unlikely. All the record tells us is that he summoned people to put the call of the Kingdom (fatherhood) of God ahead of the natural ties of family. He relativized what in the patriarchy were absolute obligations to father and family, in the name of the heavenly Father.

This paradoxical fact bears reflecting upon: Jesus neutralizes the absolute power of the earthly father by means of the claims of the heavenly Father. We could understand this to indicate that in choosing the father symbol to present the contents of God's sovereignty or kingdom Jesus wished to apply the message of grace precisely to the family situation. He might have perceived what Freud in other terms and in another time perceived, namely that the individual and therefore society are bound by the tangle of roots that tie parents and children together, that liberation must start as release from the cord of birth, and from the bondages of death. Birth and death are the two assuredly universal human experiences; all else is probably subject to cultural relativity. In his Resurrection Jesus spoke to us in the universal experience of death; in his proclamation of God's sovereign fatherhood he spoke to us at the point of birth and its aftermath—the experience of natural dependency.

The symbol of God as Father was available in his religious tradition, not prominent but nevertheless present. Jesus reached back to the level of indirect symbolization, the earlier layers of the Mosaic faith, to recover the presentation of God's sovereignty as the sovereignty of liberating love which desires free reciprocity. The impact of this proclamation was to relativize natural family relations and to constitute a new "family," the community of those who acknowledge God as Father.

One may wish that Jesus had chosen a less apparently "sexist" symbol for God. Reflection on the meaning and function of the "father" symbol, however, shows that "sexism" in the current popular sense was far from his intention in using it, and far from the inherent meaning of the symbol itself. Any hint of sexuality in the Godhead had been eliminated early on in the tradition, and the symbol "father" tends to flow into "mother" in parts of it. The effect of Jesus' using it was to deprive the patriarchy, along with everything else which is compared with the sovereignty of God, of its absolute power. The fact that Jesus chose the "father" symbol for this purpose suggests that he intended to direct his message especially at the patriarchy and to reorganize it by freeing people from its clutches. Far from being a sexist symbol, the "father" was for Jesus a weapon chosen to combat what we call "sexism." That it has been interpreted out of context to present a male god who secures the primacy of the male is a situation that might be corrected by putting it back in context as we have tried to do.

It is a possibility that Jesus chose the father symbol precisely to humanize the patriarchy, but that must remain a conjecture. What is certain, however, is that he experienced a peculiarly intimate relationship with God which made "father" the appropriate symbol of his experience. He invited his followers to share in it by giving them the privilege of invoking God as "Abba," and that privilege became the creative center of Christian worship. They participated in his spirit of sonship, but they never forgot that while his sonship was original theirs was derivative. This they signified by adapting the old idea of adoption to a new circumstance: Jesus is the "natural" son, we the adopted children. Withal, however, fatherhood and sonship symbolized the new relationship of adult freedom in union with Christ, and constituted the new family of God which was united by bonds of faith.

By now it is clear how the surface meaning of the symbol, taken as Ricoeur's streamlined version of the Oedipus complex, has enabled us to see a dimension of the biblical traditions which would otherwise have remained hidden. It has brought to light the whole nature of grace and faith as events in the realm of freedom. What, we may ask, has this deeper meaning of the symbol contributed to the surface meaning we chose? Should it be modified in any way?

In general it must be said that our method has not been optimal for the purpose of assessing the Oedipus hypothesis, because, as Ricoeur advised, we have allowed it to reveal the deeper meaning to us, and so we have seen only what it has allowed us to see. One point emerges, however, on which our evidence suggests a modification and that is that the process of negotiation from the stage of nature to the stage of freedom does not entail the kind of bitter agony and hostility that the Greek archetype of the Oedipus myth suggests. The transition can be much smoother—miraculously so, one might say. This suggests that with God there are resources for the journey from infancy to adulthood which are not available apart from him.

God the Father symbolizes grace and freedom, maturity and faith, intimacy with the divine source of life, a confidence in the final goodness of existence, the possibility of growth and creativity.

An Excursus on Method:
Symbol and History in
Modern Hermeneutics

*(with Special Reference to the
Thought of Paul Ricoeur and
Wolfhart Pannenberg)*

"Beyond the desert of criticism we wish to be called again."
                                                        —*Ricoeur.*

Since this series intends to explore new approaches to the task of
biblical theology, it is appropriate to spell out the presuppositions
which have guided the method we have used. By now it should be
apparent that we have tried to hold symbol and history together.
This is an unusual endeavor in these times when word and event
seem to have parted company in the minds of biblical interpreters.
On the one hand the heirs of the theology of the Word, especially in
its Heideggerian-Bultmannian form, have embraced a combination
of redaction criticism and literary criticism which finds the events
that gave rise to the gospel texts of little interest. In the words of
Robin Scroggs,

> This new perspective emphasizes the creative influence of the final
> author upon the gospel tradition, such that even the "historical" resi-
> due form critics found in the Gospels is being called into question.
> Indeed, one can today find researchers who claim the burden of proof
> to be upon those who assert the reliability and detectability of any
> pre-gospel traditions. From this perspective the Gospels are theological-
> literary tracts dating from A.D. 70–100, and the Church behind the
> Gospels, let alone the historical Jesus, becomes a murky, indistinct
> figure.[1]

1. "A New Old Quest? A Review Essay," *JAAR* 40 (1972) 506.

Critics of this persuasion are producing literary analyses of the texts using structuralism, linguistics, and methods of aesthetic analysis.[2]

On the other hand, some, like the present author, still maintain that the history behind the text is the determinative part of the biblical phenomenon; and although we find it harsh to be called "the attack from the right," we are content with the "moderately conservative" epithet, awarded this position by Norman Perrin.[3]

Fortunately each side of the dichotomy has a representative of great brilliance and sensitivity whose insight transcends the squabbling of the less gifted; we mean Paul Ricoeur as a representative of the former position, and Wolfhart Pannenberg of the latter. Our discussion of method will take the form of a brief comparison of the thought of these two men and an endeavor to show from their thought how, at the highest level of reflection, symbol and history (word and event), which lesser minds put asunder, are joined together. We begin with a brief orientation to the current hermeneutical discussion.

THE RECENT HERMENEUTICAL DISCUSSION

Stendahl's article on biblical theology in the *Interpreter's Dictionary of the Bible* (1962)[4] is a good guide to the discussion up until the end of the "fifties." Briefly, the decisive factor in biblical scholarship since the triumph of the critical method in the nineteenth century is the work of the "history of religions" school (*Religionsgeschichtlicheschule*). It treats the biblical text as an historical document firmly attached to the times and places of its provenance, and thereby opens a great chasm of discontinuity between the thoughts and beliefs of the Bible and those of the modern world. The most striking example of this effect is the portrayal of Jesus by Johannes Weiss[5] and Albert Schweitzer[6] as one enmeshed in the skein of out-

---

2. See the periodical *Semeia*, published by the Society of Biblical Literature. Its declaration of policy includes the following: "Studies employing the methods, models, and findings of linguistics, folklore studies, contemporary literary criticism, structuralism, social anthropology, and other such disciplines and approaches, are invited."

3. Norman Perrin, *Rediscovering*, 223–4.

4. "Biblical Theology," IDB, II, 418–432, esp. p. 418.

5. *Jesus' Proclamation of the Kingdom of God*, trans. Hiers and Holland (Philadelphia: Fortress, 1971; first edition, 1892).

6. *The Quest of the Historical Jesus*, trans. W. Montgomery (New York: Macmillan, 1961; first edition, 1906).

landish imagery and expectation which was Jewish apocalyptic. Jesus did not exemplify the genteel equanimity of a middle-class moralist, pledged to the fatherhood of God, the brotherhood of man and the infinite worth of the individual soul, as Harnack's distillation of Christian essence averred;[7] rather, he was obsessed with the imminent end of the world, to be effected by the miraculous appearance of a new order of existence, called "the Kingdom of God." Jesus belongs to "another world," and so do all the biblical witnesses. If they are to be taken seriously as guides to the nature of things, it must be demonstrated that they are not made obsolete by the passage of time. This is, indeed, what the church claims to have demonstrated, but we cannot base our case on the church's claims alone; we must show reasonable grounds for regarding the biblical traditions as believable guides to the nature of things. Theological hermeneutics endeavors to bridge the gap separating the Bible from the modern world, and thus to understand the biblical message for our time.

Generally speaking, interpreters are divided into two camps: those who find the constitutive content of the biblical message in the events and persons about which the text testifies, and those who find this content in the testimonies as such. This distinction between event and testimony might seem unnecessarily fastidious, but it does have good reason behind it. Historical analysis showed that several of the "events" are unlikely to have occurred as reported, and so in these cases we have accounts of what the writers believed or hoped might have happened, rather than of what actually happened; accounts that tell us about the convictions or delusions of the writers, rather than about the actual happenings. The miracle stories are, of course, the most vivid instances of this interpretative problem. The concept of the relationship between event and testimony is complex, and we cannot present a history of the discussion here. A brief sketch of general hermeneutical trends will, however, serve to introduce our more systematic proposals.

We begin with the interpreters who find the Bible's constitutive element in the testimony rather than in the events testified to, because in recent discussion the term "hermeneutics" has been used

---

7. Adolf Harnack, *What is Christianity?* trans. T. B. Saunders (New York: Harpers, 1957; originally delivered as lectures in the University of Berlin in 1899–1900).

chiefly to describe the endeavors of these "theologians of the Word" to translate that word for our time.[8] Bultmann's "demythologizing" proposal is the most famous instance of this enterprise. Whatever the precise nature of the event or person might have been, the biblical witness interprets it from the point of view of faith in God. This interpretation is the constitutive content of the Bible and is timeless, as God is above time, and as faith in God is a perpetual possibility. Indeed, the operative content of the Bible is the faith of its witnesses rather than the events which lie behind that faith; such history as it contains is the "history" of "supra-historical" faith.

Bultmann understood this faith to be a mode of understanding the self—the self as structured by dependence on God. From the "common-sense" point of view, for which events in the public domain—wars, treaties, migrations—are an ineluctable element in history, the theology of the Word cut the historical moorings of biblical faith and set it adrift on the ocean of ideas. Bultmann's tribute to tradition in the form of a redefinition of historicity—as the self's openness to the future—merely emphasizes the severance between public events and private. Although much "happens" in the life of a Bultmannian believer, it is only randomly related to the public events of which the Bible speaks, or indeed, to the current external circumstances of the believer. Schubert Ogden suggests,[9] with some plausibility, that the *kerygma*—Bultmann's term for the possibility of authentic existence (or life in faith)—is, by Bultmann's logic, only arbitrarily based on the historical figure of Jesus; in principle this authentic existence is available to anyone who understands its terms, whether they know of Jesus or not. It must be said, however, that the *kerygma* is historically if not necessarily attached to Jesus, and that Bultmann did honor contingency in this instance; whether such regard was inconsistent with his ontology, as Ogden suggests, cannot be settled here. This much is clear, however; for Bultmann the content of the Bible is the pattern of response by the biblical witnesses, and this pattern, called *kerygma*, is the offer of the possibility of a certain self-understanding.

In its New Testament form the *kerygma* occurs in a symbolic

---

8. See Perrin, *Rediscovering*, 207–248.
9. *Christ Without Myth, A Study based on the Theology of Rudolf Bultmann* (New York: Harpers, 1961).

language, which Bultmann calls myth. The New Testament writers might have regarded this language as literal, but for us it is symbolic, and so can be "translated" or, in more flamboyant idiom, "demythologized." When the biblical message is properly translated into the language of our time, we can hear, understand and respond to it, recapitulate in ourselves the structure of existence which it recommends, and with good conscience worship the Bible's God. Thus the theology of the Word overcame the barrier of strangeness which the historical method had discovered between us and the Bible. It did not so much find a way through the "desert of criticism" as fly right over it. By locating the Bible's constitutive content in the subjectivity of the witnesses it made the faith immune to criticism based on "external history."

In its second generation the theology of the Word showed signs of uneasiness about its ahistoricity, with Ebeling interpreting the historical Jesus as an exemplar of faith, a faith which we might repeat, and Fuchs pointing us to the deeds of Jesus as part of the proclamation of the *kerygma*—all the while, however, teasing out a hybrid category "Word-event," whose obscurities need not detain us here. Käsemann insisted most passionately that there should be a demonstrable congruence between the historical Jesus and proclaimed Christ.[10]

Now the theology of the Word is entering a third stage of major influence in a form peculiar to America, as the "literary" interpretation of the Bible—to be distinguished from "the Bible as literature." In the hands of such people as Robert Funk,[11] Dominic Crossan,[12] Robert Tannehill[13] and the late Norman Perrin,[14] the interpretation of New Testament texts as literary artifacts patient of analysis by means that might be termed "aesthetic," in a broad sense, goes ahead. The dean of this school, if it may be called one, is Amos

10. Perrin, *Rediscovering.*
11. E.g. *Language, Hermeneutic and Word of God, The Problem of Language in the New Testament and Contemporary Theology* (New York: Harpers, 1966) ; Funk is the moving force behind the journal *Semeia.*
12. *In Parables, The Challenge of the Historical Jesus* (New York; Harpers, 1973) .
13. *The Sword of His Mouth,* Semeia Supplements (Philadelphia: Fortress and Missoula: Scholar's, 1975) .
14. *Jesus and the Language of the Kingdom, Symbol and Metaphor in New Testament Interpretation* (Philadelphia: Fortress, 1976) .

Wilder,[15] and Dan Via's work[16] on the parables did much to make its aspirations known. The most considerable intellect ranged on its side, however, is Paul Ricoeur, although his thought is too powerful to be confined in one camp, as we hope to show in what follows. He declares that philosophy in general is a hermeneutics—a translator of obscure texts, written and unwritten.[17] He is in search of a general theory of language as part of the quest for a general hermeneutics of reality, and has at his command the resources of psychoanalysis, phenomenology, and modern linguistic philosophy, as well as his own concrete reflection. Ricoeur's thought will be our initial guide into the question of the nature of symbolism and the relationship between symbol and event.

RICOEUR ON SYMBOLS AND HISTORY

For Ricoeur a symbol is a device for bringing experience to the level of definition at which it becomes available to thought.[18] It is not unexpected, therefore, when he welcomes Bultmann's demythologizing of the *kerygma*; for as long as the proclamation is treated as a quasi-literal explanation of who Christ is and what salvation is, the symbols contained in the myth are in bondage to a false end and therefore cannot function to bring experience to thought. The false end to which they are shackled is explanation. When that pseudo-logos is expelled from the myth and it ceases to be an explanation, the symbols are set free to give their meaning, free for what Ricoeur calls "poiesis." Bultmann understood demythologization to be a translation of the *kerygma* into nonsymbolic terms; he favored the existentialist categories of Heidegger's early philosophy and accepted as an alternative to "demythologization" the phrase "an existentialist interpretation." Ricoeur emphatically affirms the perdurability of the symbols after demythologization, and so differs from Bultmann in this important respect. For Ricoeur demythologization is a liberation of the symbols from a spurious logos, imposed

---

15. *The Language of the Gospels: Early Christian Rhetoric* (New York: Harper & Row, 1964).

16. *The Parables, Their Literary and Existential Dimension* (Philadelphia: Fortress, 1967).

17. Don Ihde, *Hermeneutic Phenomenology: The Philosophy of Paul Ricoeur* (Evanston: Northwestern University, 1971).

18. *The Symbolism of Evil.*

by the myth, so that they might give to thought their true meaning, not the translation of symbols into some nonsymbolic language.

Thus it is that symbols are the point of departure for reflection, for the symbol is a mask, an expression of double meaning which demands deciphering and gives rise to thought. Ricoeur gives both a broad and a narrow definition of symbol. Broadly speaking, "a symbol exists . . . where linguistic expression lends itself by its double or multiple meanings to a work of interpretation."[19] In practise Ricoeur does not limit the definition to "linguistic expression": he treats existence in all of its manifestations—dreams, ideals, rituals—as a text to be interpreted. Indeed, the need for interpretation is the clue to the presence of the symbolic; opacity entails hermeneutics. Nevertheless, this broad definition does not take us as far as Cassirer's contention that all understanding is symbolic because the very process by which thought orders and gives meaning to the world of experience is a constructing of symbols. There are nonsymbolic statements, as there are also special concentrations of opacity and multivalency which are symbols in the narrow sense. Ricoeur offers the symbols of evil as an example of this narrower definition. The series of symbols, stain—defilement—guilt, shows how an experience (fault) is symbolized initially (stain) and then how symbols interpret each other (defilement, guilt) and finally give rise to reflective thought.

The experience (fault) is inaccessible to thought except through the symbolic series. For this reason symbols are the creatures of need, expressions of our exigency in the face of life's depth. Freud too regarded symbols as a confession of need; for him they are substitutes for an honesty that we cannot stand, euphemisms for the intolerable truth of the atavism of desire. The Freudian anthropologist Robert Paul refers to the "ultimate falseness of the symbolic world,"[20] a falseness which causes us anxiety, because symbols make up the fabric of culture which falls like a curtain between us and the natural rhythms of our bodies. For Freud symbols are badges of psychic servitude, to be stripped by analysis. For Jung, on the contrary, they are the great reconcilers and revealers; by revealing the

---

19. *Freud and Philosophy, An Essay on Interpretation,* trans. by Denis Savage (New Haven and London: Yale University, 1971) 18.
20. Robert Paul, "Did the Primal Crime take place?" *Ethos* 4 (1976) 311–352, 340.

unconscious and its roots in a common field of universal significance, the symbol reconciles the conscious and the unconscious,
thereby transforming the person into a unified self. Ricoeur stands
somewhere between the two great analysts: his symbols do, indeed,
reveal by a process that might be compared to Jung's understanding
of the symbol's function. However, it is to Freud that Ricoeur looks
for guidance, because of the relative austerity of Freud's thought,
which operates with a few basic assumptions—viz. desire and its
resistances—in interpreting culture. Ricoeur believes that symbols
donate to thought its point of departure; starting with symbols
properly interpreted, thought is to go on to articulated understanding; symbols provide the impulse to philosophy. For Jung, symbols
are substitutes for reflective reasoning; for Freud, symbols are ob-
stacles to reflective reasoning; for Ricoeur symbols are the opportunity and the impulse to reflective reasoning.

For symbols to be the impulse to such reasoning they must be
properly interpreted. This takes place when we pass from the literal
(surface) to the analogical (deep) meaning of the symbol, not by a
process of logical thought external to the relationship between the
perceiver and the symbol, but rather by an "assimilation" to the
latent meaning by a "dwelling in" the literal. The symbol, therefore, is "donative"; it gives its latent meaning "by grace and not by
works."[21] The appropriation of that meaning by the subject must be
watched over by a "hermeneutics of suspicion" in the light of an
"archaeology of the subject" laid bare by means of Freudian instru-
mentality. By this means desire's strategy to distort meaning to satisfy its boundless narcissism can be contained, and self-deception
kept at a minimum.

Ricoeur bases his conviction that such a deep meaning exists
in the symbol on his confidence in the donative resources of
language, on

> the belief that language, which bears symbols, is not so much spoken
> by men as spoken to men; that men are born into language, into the
> light of the logos "who enlightens every man who comes into the
> world."[22]

21. *Symbolism of Evil,* 15–16; *Freud and Philosophy,* 17.
22. *Freud and Philosophy,* 29.

Thus he subscribes to the "high" view of language which is characteristic of the theology of the Word, especially in the thought of Ebeling and Fuchs, the so-called "New Hermeneutic." There are good grounds outside of the theological circle for such a view of language, as the work of such linguists as Chomsky, anthropologists such as Lévi-Strauss, and psychoanalysts such as Jacques Lacan shows. It cannot be seriously doubted that language is a donor of structure and meaning to existence, and that there is a reciprocity of action between what is spoken and the speaker. To paraphrase Winston Churchill on the subject of the architecture of the new House of Commons, "We form ur buildings and our buildings form us." Thus it is with language.

The power of language to shape existence tempts us to an inflated view of it, however. The theology of the Word succumbed in part to this temptation, making language the sole bearer of significance, and neglecting the events which impinge on life and help to shape its meaning, events which call forth language and which language interprets. Aware of this danger, Ricoeur invites us to practice a "hermeneutics of suspicion." Since the generosity of language encourages a "hermeneutics of manifestation" by which the fading significance of debilitated symbols is rejuvenated, the temptation for those who grasp this generosity is great. Ricoeur would have us receive the "gift" of meaning which the symbol has to give, but he would prevent us from hypostatizing language, from idolizing a symbol. Thus he writes: "In our time we have not finished doing away with idols and we have barely begun to listen to symbols."[23] A hermeneutics of suspicion must accompany any interpretative endeavor which is to meet reasonable canons of truth. We must not demythify, but we must demythologize if we are to demystify; and we cannot recover the abundant meaning of symbols without this ascesis, because of the false consciousness each one is heir to.

The theme of "false consciousness" takes us to the heart of Ricoeur's attempt to repristinate reflective philosophy as a hermeneutics. Reflective philosophy is the travail to possess the self; reflection is a "re-appropriation of our effort to exist."[24] Descartes

23. *Ibid.*, 27.
24. *Ibid.*, 45

believed that the *cogito* was the unassailable self in its concentrated significance. Nietzsche, Marx, and Freud have shown that the *cogito,* while it might be the self as posited, is not the self possessed; it is the fact but not the truth of consciousness. The Cartesian thinks that in consciousness meaning and the consciousness of meaning coincide. The three "masters of suspicion," Nietzsche, Marx, and Freud, cast doubt on consciousness' ability to know directly the meaning of things. "Henceforward, to seek meaning is no longer to spell out the consciousness of meaning, but to decipher its expressions."[25] In short, I am not who I think I am, and things are not what they seem to be. "In and through man desires advance masked,"[26] and the task of philosophy is to grapple behind the mask with the hidden desires which distort meaning, since to unmask them is impossible. According to the three great "demystifiers" consciousness is deceived by hidden forces—the will to power, social being, unconscious desires—which encode meaning; a "mediate science of meaning" must match the coding skill of its hidden adversary. Guile must be met with guile. Ricoeur rejects Husserlian phenomenology because it is not suspicious enough of consciousness' ability to discern meaning; indeed, it is posited on the ability of the knower to apprehend the meaning of the known directly.

Symbols are the foundation stones of thought; but their dark side rests not only on the barren sands of duplicity but also in the fertile soil of hope; and hope is informed by memory. The deep meaning of a symbol always has two vectors, like memory and hope, archaeology of the subject and teleology of the subject, Freud and Hegel. If the symbol is embedded in memory and hope, it is embedded in history; it points backwards and forwards along the time-line, and not off into an umbilical ocean or up to a celestial warehouse of ideas. Its analogous meaning is always historical, that is, part of experience. It has two vectors which correspond to the archaeology and teleology of the self respectively; it recalls childhood and explores adulthood, it looks backwards and it anticipates.[27] We reserve the term "symbol" for this historically

25. *Ibid.,* 33.
26. *Ibid.,* 162.
27. *Ibid.,* 496.

rooted phenomenon. *A symbol is a unit of sense with a double meaning, whose "other" meaning is always historical in the sense that it explores hope by means of reminiscence and memory by means of anticipation.*

This is our definition, not Ricoeur's, although it is obviously indebted to him. We give much more weight to the historical nature of experience than Ricoeur does explicitly. He speaks more of the semantic function of symbol than we do, and therefore is claimed by those who regard the word as primary in hermeneutics rather than the experience which it describes.

The symbolism of evil exemplifies our definition; it presents "the experience of fault" which although it cannot be conceptualized except by means of symbols initially, nevertheless was "experienced" and is remembered as part of that human experience called history. Freud recognized the importance of history; to the dismay of many disciples he interpreted ethnological material to show that a primal parricide had taken place; and he insisted to the end of his life on this account of the primal crime. He believed the whole structure of psychoanalysis as a metapsychology rested on this event. He understood that without a commonly experienced event to account for the Oedipal situation in the individual and in society, he was at the mercy of metaphysics, or worse, a theology based on the same. Our option is like his, either memory or metaphysics.

PANNENBERG ON HISTORY AND HERMENEUTICS

In choosing memory and hope, we align ourselves with those who find the center of gravity of the biblical message to lie in the events rather than in the witness to those events. On this view the excesses of symbolic interpretation are curbed by the facts of history, as well as by a Freudian hermeneutical suspicion. Wolfhart Pannenberg speaks most authoritatively for this position today. For him, the revelation of God takes place in the events which lie as cause and referent, behind the biblical texts.[28] The teaching of Jesus is part of that history, and from his proclamation of the Kingdom's imminent advent we learn most easily that his people

---

28. *Revelation as History*, ed. Wolfhart Pannenberg, trans. David Granskow (London: Macmillan, 1968).

understood their history to be a history of the fulfillment of God's promise. The promise of the imminent Kingdom was fulfilled for Jesus in his Resurrection, which is, in turn, a revelation of the fulfillment in store for all history. Thus the Bible makes these two major claims, that the fundamental nature of reality is historical, and that history has meaning. God is that which determines every existing thing as part of a reality in process of change through time; so to understand the direction of history is to understand God's self-revelation. The goal of the process is its transformation, as revealed in Jesus' Resurrection; so to know the Resurrection is to know the goal and therefore the direction of history, which is to know God in his self-revelation.

Since the modern understanding of reality is historical, the bridge between the biblical past and the modern present is the experience of reality as historical. We share a common understanding with the Bible; not merely a self-understanding but rather an understanding of reality and, potentially, of God's revelation in this reality. The experience of reality as contingent and changing is the same today as it was in biblical times, and so the "horizon" of our modern consciousness, to use Gadamer's image, and the horizon of biblical consciousness are taken up into the larger horizon of the historical process, and thus unified. We experience life in the same way as the Bible did, as contingent and fragmentary, exigent and open to a meaning from the future. This historical understanding of reality was as surprising in biblical times, when surrounding cultures saw the real as structured and enduring, as was the Bible's assertion that history has a meaning. Today the contingency of all things is a common assumption; that this contingency has meaning is not so commonly assumed; that its meaning is the transformation previewed in the Resurrection of Jesus is the conviction of relatively few. Nevertheless, this does seem to be the message of the Bible, and whether it convinces many or few, Pannenberg is right in presenting it as the Christian faith.

For Pannenberg this hermeneutical bridge of a common experience of the world as historical is essentially an experience of God as the "all-determining reality."[29] God, therefore, is the one who

---

29. *Wissenschaftstheorie und Theologie* (Frankfurt-am-Main: Suhrkamp, 1973) 426. E.T. *Theology and the Philosophy of Science,* trans. F. McDonagh (Philadelphia: Westminster, 1976) 424. Our references are to the original text.

binds past and present together as the hypothetical principle of history's wholeness; and God must remain an hypothesis because, for us, history is not yet over, and the truth about a process can be assuredly known only when it is complete. Hence theology cannot be delivered from controversy.[30] In the meantime a particular period of history can be interrogated about the presence in it of the all-determining reality, and when this is discovered it serves as the basis upon which the period of the interrogator and the period interrogated can be brought together to illuminate one another. So history is the history of the manifestation of God's reality as well as humanity's.[31]

This view is not a repristination of the theory of an "essence of Christianity." God as the all-determining reality is not an idea to be abstracted from the course of history. Revelation is not a pattern of ideas delivered in history, but is the course of history itself understood by means of the principle inherent in it, namely historical contingency, which in turn, entails the awareness of a non-contingent whole. In this line of argument Pannenberg sees himself developing Schleiermacher's analysis of religion as the "intuition and consciousness of the universal,"[32] which, in turn, goes back to F. H. Jacobi. Jacobi argues that we cannot have the consciousness of finite things without at the same time experiencing an intuition of the infinite. Schleiermacher sought to combine this view with a modified—to exclude pantheism—Spinozaist idea of the presence of the infinite in the finite. The finite is constituted by the limits which set it apart from the infinite, therefore the finite can only be fully understood within the context of the infinite. Religious consciousness views reality within this larger context and so is a richer and truer mode of perception than the secular. In developing this line of thought, Pannenberg argues that we have more than merely an intuition of the whole since history itself has given a preview and

---

30. "Dass Theologie die göttliche als die alles bestimmende Wirklichkeit in ihrer Strittigkeit zum Gegenstand hat, das hängt damit zusammen, dass die Wirklichkeit im ganzen noch unabgeschlossen ist," *ibid.* "Theology's concern with the divine as all-determining reality as a matter of dispute is connected with the fact that reality as a whole is still incomplete" (ET, 424).

31. ". . . die Erscheinungsgeschichte der Wirklichkeit Gottes, wie auch des Menschen . . ." *ibid.*, 425. ". . . it is concerned in the history of religion with the history of the apparition of the reality of God as well as that of man" (ET, 423).

32. *Ibid.*, 371.

anticipatory experience of it in the Resurrection of Jesus. The Resurrection is not an idea or declaration of faith, but an event to be investigated and initially understood by historical methods. Thus the meaning of history as a whole is given within history; but only as an hypothesis, or hope, since history is not yet over.

Pannenberg's hermeneutics makes it impossible to elevate a symbol above history so that it becomes equally meaningful in whatever period, as if it were an essential idea. Its meaning is determined by its place in the history of traditions. Nevertheless we can interrogate a symbol about its relationship to the all-determining reality as that is present in the history in which the symbol is located. In this sense we have tried to understand the "father" symbol in the world of the New Testament and in our contemporary world. To put the matter bluntly, we have asked what it tells us about God.

We chose to interrogate this specific image not because it commends itself on philosophic or psychoanalytical grounds, although those grounds are firm and fruitful, but because of its historical grounds; because throughout Christian history it has been and continues to be a central symbol for the Christian experience of God. It was in fact a crucial part of Jesus' experience of God and it remains so for contemporary Christians. That it is being challenged by certain Christian feminists as discriminatory against the female sex makes this an urgent undertaking. Before we can come to terms with the merits of that challenge we have to know what the "father" symbol means within Christian history, and, of course, the challenge itself is part of that history and, therefore, one of the factors determining that meaning. Ideally we should study the symbol as it occurs in all Christian history; that we treat only the biblical and the current periods is a testimony to infirmity, and to the hitherto imperfect conception of the theological task, embalmed in the disciplinary subdivisions of the field. In short, we are taking up Pannenberg's challenge to leave behind the division between "scientific history" which excludes the God hypothesis, and kerygmatic theology, which enshrines God within an impenetrable fortress of subjective affirmation, and to interpret two historical periods—the biblical and the modern—by asking about their relationship to God, as the all-determining reality, using the symbol "father" as a point on which to focus.

CONVERGENCES BETWEEN THE THOUGHT
OF PANNENBERG AND RICOEUR

There are some notable convergences between the thought of Pannenberg and Ricoeur, which are important for us. We have already seen that in Ricoeur's view symbol demands an historical rootage. In a remarkable essay on structuralism,[33] he compares von Rad's description of Israel's understanding of reality with Lévi-Strauss's structuralism. For the latter, the abstract structure of language provides a pattern into which cultures can be fitted; synchronicity takes precedence over diachronicity; the coming to be of things is merely a disturbance in the otherwise tranquil permanence of the structure. For Ricoeur, von Rad's exposition of Israel's historical traditions provides a convincing alternative to structuralism. The traditions are interpretations that receive their impulse and their content "from a network of signifying events" which generates an "initial surplus of meaning which motivates tradition and interpretation."[34] This last stage is that of the "historicity of hermeneutics" which, we may infer, is still our situation, excepting that we have two millenia of hermeneutical historicity between us and the redactors of scripture. We still have to interpret history from within history; even that interpretation of the biblical history called theology is subject to the vagaries of time; there is no final theology, only the history of theology as an account of our memory and anticipation, our faith and our hope. There could scarcely be a stronger affirmation of the event-related historicity of biblical religion than this; Pannenberg and Ricoeur converge in their mutual dependence on von Rad. Whether Ricoeur's identification of the historicity of hermeneutics in the Old Testament can be taken by inference, as we have taken it, to mean that he, like Pannenberg, would see such historicity as our situation too, within a common horizon of historical process which we share with the biblical writers, is uncertain. Nevertheless, it is a fair inference.

For Pannenberg the discontinuity between our world and the Bible's is not total because we share with the Bible the experience of reality as historical. However, the Bible's explanation of our historicity as the experience of the acting God (the all-determining

33. "Structure and Hermeneutics," trans. Kathleen McLaughlin, in *The Conflict of Interpretations,* 27–61.
34. *Ibid.,* 48.

reality), of the meaning of history as transformation through Resurrection, is by no means widely shared today. Pannenberg however holds that these explanations should be accepted because, amongst other things, like the historical evidence for the Resurrection, they make sense out of our experience of reality. Ricoeur uses a similar method which he calls "a transcendental deduction of symbols."[35] Although Pannenberg would object to any suggestion of a transcendent structure of thought, his methods if not his presuppositions are similar to Ricoeur's. In the case of the myths symbolizing evil, Ricoeur chooses one as revealed, and therefore true, on the basis of its power to reveal. Its power to reveal is tested by committing myself to it in a wager that it will reveal me to myself by means of "a qualitative transformation of reflexive consciousness." This maneuver is an instance of the hermeneutical circle which in its theological form is: that in order to understand one must believe, but before one can believe one must understand. By committing oneself to a myth in order to test its revealing power, one is believing in order to understand. For Ricoeur, however, believing has the nature of a wager, and is therefore experimental and tentative; he also describes it as "living in the aura of meaning" of the myth in question; there is nothing irrevocable about the believing. Here is a form of the *crede ut intelligas* which corresponds to the method of argument used by Pannenberg—believe the biblical explanations because and as long as they are able to make sense out of our experience!

BIBLICAL SYMBOLS AS TRANSLATORS OF HISTORY

Thus both Ricoeur and Pannenberg traverse the hermeneutical gap in the same way, by finding material from "then" that makes sense out of "now." For Ricoeur the test case is the symbolism of evil, while for Pannenberg it is the Resurrection, which is, as a term, also symbol. The nature of this material is of linguistic sense units with double meaning, the symbols of evil on the one hand, and the Resurrection—which means literally "awaking from sleep"— on the other. The impulse for the formation of these symbols comes

---

35. *Symbolism of Evil*, 353–5.

originally from historical experience, from "hidden time" as Ricoeur calls the deep level of historicity,[36] which is inaccessible to thought except by way of symbol. This inaccessibility of "hidden time" is especially vivid in the case of the Resurrection; without the symbol all we can say is, "He is not here."

The myth of the Fall and the accounts of the Resurrection are symbolic in having "another" meaning that arises out of memory and hope, a meaning which we come to know by living in the literal meaning and being assimilated thereby to the analogical meaning. The memory of deep meaning which the symbol recalls is similar, and different, in the case of the Fall and the Resurrection respectively. It is similar as an historical experience, different in relative time-boundedness; the experience of fault takes place for each one of us at one time or another, and the myth of the Fall fixes it at a hypothetical moment; the Resurrection took place for Jesus at a fixed moment and the symbol makes it available to us at one time or another. So the two symbols move between "then" and "now," bringing us gifts of meaning, gifts of opposite effect: the one attaches a general experience to a specific event, the other makes a specific event generally available to experience. Therefore, biblical symbols are revealers of the depths of meaning in history not guides to psychic mysteries; in the biblical sphere they reveal what is remembered and what is hoped for from the experience of history as the work of God. They are one of the ways in which history manifests itself as related to the all-determining reality, God.

We have tried to show what the symbol "Father" reveals of history as the manifestation of God. Our investigations have shown that it identifies those forces in history which liberate the self from irrational bondage and make possible a free and responsible selfhood. This free responsibility for the self in relation to God is called faith. It was exemplified by Jesus, and the good news of the gospel is that it is possible for everyone. Properly understood, therefore, the biblical symbol "Father" means virtually the opposite of what the radical feminists understand it to mean, freedom not bondage, responsibility not dependence, adulthood not infantilism.

---

36. *Ibid.,* 46.

In the historicity of hermeneutics, however, their challenge to theology has enabled us to understand this dimension of the symbol. It remains for the church to make this newly understood "fatherhood" central to its understanding of God, and of human fatherhood. Then we will have taken a giant step away from patriarchy and towards mutuality.

Indexes

AUTHORS, EDITORS, AND TRANSLATORS

SCRIPTURE REFERENCES

EARLY JEWISH SOURCES

Tobit
13:4 — 54

Wisdom of Solomon
2:16 — 54
11:10 — 54
14:3 — 54

Sirach
23:1 — 54
23:4 — 54
51:10 — 54

Dead Sea Scrolls
1 QH 9:35ff. — 54

2 Enoch
100:2 — 67

Jer. Sota
19a, 8 — 55

Joseph and Asenath
12:14 — 54

Book of Jubilees
1:24 — 54
1:28 — 54
19:29 — 54

3 Maccabees
5:7 — 54
6:3 — 54
7:6 — 54

Pirke Aboth
1:5 — 56

Sifra Leviticus
20:26 — 54, 77

Tannith
2a — 95

Tg. Yer. Lev.
22:28 — 54

Sanhedrin
99b — 88

Str-B
III, 341 — 88
III, 559 — 88